Boise
Trail Guide

75

Hiking & Running Routes
Close to Home

By Steve Stuebner

Acknowledgments

I want to thank all of the people who helped me with this project. In particular, I want to thank Maggie Lawrence and the Boise Bs, Lynette McDougal and Tricia Keener Blaha from the Hash House Harriers, Frank Billue, and Leo Hennessy, Mr. Idaho Outdoors extraordinaire, for logging routes for me. I want to thank Steve Blake and Mike Carlson at Boise RunWalk for their tips. I want to thank Shu at Idaho Running Company and Gregg at Bandanna Running and Walking for providing feedback on the hike/run list and for advertising in the book. I want to thank National Geographic TOPO! for giving permission to use their electronic base maps and profiles. And most of all, I want to thank my partner Wendy and our family for their patience and support.

Credits

•**Cover and back cover photos** by Glenn Oakley, www.oakleyphoto.com
•**Cover design**: Sally Stevens, www.idea-monger.com
•**Proof-reading**: Kim Lock
•**All base maps** created with TOPO! ©2006 National Geographic
•**All elevation profiles** created TOPO! ©2006 National Geographic
To learn more visit: http://www.nationalgeographic.com/topo

See www.stevestuebner.com for Steve's other books

Salmon River Country
Paddling the Payette, 3rd edition
Mountain Biking in Boise, 4th edition
Mountain Biking in McCall, 2nd edition
Mountain Biking Idaho Falcon Guide
Discover Idaho's Centennial Trail
Cool North Wind: Morley Nelson's Life with Birds of Prey

Table of Contents

Master Map 5
Introduction 7
Hiking and Running Tips 8
About public land agencies 10
Annual Calendar of Events for run/walk events 12
Photo Gallery 14
Race to Robie Creek, the toughest half-marathon in the Northwest 18
Training tips for Race to Robie Creek 21
How to hook up with local hiking/running groups 23

Greenbelt Trails 26

1. Eagle Greenbelt to Riverside Park 28
2. Veterans Park to Glenwood 30
3. Veterans Park - Garden City Loop 32
4. Veterans Park Pond Loop 34
5. Greenbelt Undperpass Special 36
6. Capital to ParkCenter Loop 38
7. Municipal Park to Barber Park Loop 40
8. Barber Park to River Run walking path 42
9. Kathryn Albertson Park Loop 44
10. Eckert Road to Lucky Peak 46
11. Nampa Greenbelt 48
12. Caldwell Greenbelt 50

Easy Mountain Trails 52

13. Big Springs - Veterans Loop 54
14. Seaman's Gulch Double Loop 56
15. Camelsback Kids Special 58
16. Red Fox - Owls Roost 60
17. Military Reserve Easy Double Loop 62
18. Castle Rock Loop 64
19. Surprise Valley - Oregon Trail Loop 66
20. Quickest way to Heaven at Bogus Basin 68
21. Beaver Creek - Crooked River Loop 70
22. Cougar Loop - Lehn's Loop (Park 'n Ski Trails) 72
23. Blue Lake Family Special 74
24. Bruneau Sand Dunes 76
25. Jump Creek Canyon 78

Moderate Mountain Trails 80

26. Eagle Foothills Little Gulch Loop 82
27. Hidden Springs Redtail Ridge Loop 84
28. Polecat Gulch Finger Ridge Loop 86
29. Corrals - Bob's Loop 88
30. Corrals - Hulls - Camelsback Loop 90
31. Dry Creek out and back 92
32. Kestrel-Red Cliffs Loop 94

Moderate Mountain Trails (cont.)

33. Crestline "Freeway" - Hulls Loop 96
34. Military Reserve Double Ridge Loop 98
35. Military Reserve Two Coyote Loop 100
36. Shane's Loop 102
37. Orchard Gulch - Five Mile Creek 104
38. Explore Turner Gulch 106
39. Bogus Basin Contour Special 108
40. Mores Mountain Loop 110
41. Idaho City - Charcoal Gulch Loop 112
42. Banner Ridge - Alpine - Elkhorn Loop 114
43. Station Creek Loops 116
44. Halverson Lake Loop 118
45. Wildcat Canyon Loop 120
46. Reynolds Creek Loop 122
47. Leslie Gulch - Juniper Gulch Scramble 124

Strenuous Mountain Trails 126

48. Hillside to the Hollow 128
49. Corrals to Corrals Loop 130
50. Crestline - Sidewinder Loop 132
51. Hulls - Sidewinder Loop 134
52. Hulls Gulch Interpretive Trail 136
53. Camelsback - Hulls - Bob's Shuttle 138
54. Jumpin' Jeepers Figure 8 Loop 140
55. Miltiary Reserve - Sidewinder Loop 142
56. Three Bears Loop 144
57. Foothills on the Rocks (Table Rock) 146
58. Candyland Table Rock Loop 148
59-60. Squaw Creek Loops 150
61. Twin Peaks at Bogus Basin Loop 152
62. Cottonwood Creek out and back 154
63. Pilot Peak out and back 156
64. Sunset Lookout out and back 158
65. Zimmer Creek Loop 160
66. Tripod Peak out and back 162
67. One Spoon Steepness 164
68. Snake River Petroglyph Tour 166

Epic Mountain Trails 168

69. Boise Ridge Climber's Special 170
70. Stueby's Death March 172
71. Race to Robie Creek course 174
72. Rocky Canyon - Trail #4 Loop 176
73. Squaw Creek - Trail #8 - Trail E Loop 178
74. Thorn Butte - Cottonwood Creek Loop 180
75. Wilson Creek - Mini Moab Loop 182

Advertising Gallery 184

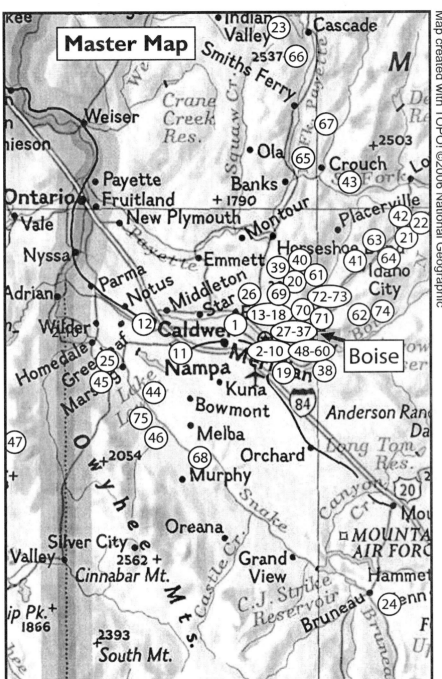

Master Map

Indian Valley
Cascade
23
Smiths Ferry
2537 66
Crane Creek Res.
Weiser
67
hieson
2503
Ola
65
Crouch
Payette
Fruitland
Banks
43
Ontario
+1790
New Plymouth
Montour
Placerville
42 22
Vale
63 21
Nyssa
Emmett
Horseshoe
40 41 64
39 20 61
Idano City
Parma
Middleton
26 69 72-73
Notus
Star
13-18 70 71
Adrian
12
Caldwe
1
27-37
62 74
11
2-10 48-60
Boise
Wilder
25
Nampa
19 38
Homedale
45
Kuna
Gree
84
44
Bowmont
Anderson Ran
Da
2054
75
Melba
Long Tom Res.
47
46
Orchard
68
Murphy
20
Mou
Oreana
MOUNTA
AIR FOR
Silver City
2562
Grand View
Hammet
Valley
Cinnabar Mt.
C.J. Strike Reservoir
Bruneau
24
ip Pk.
1866
2393
South Mt.

Disclaimer

Warning: HIKING AND TRAIL RUNNING INVOLVE A NUMBER OF RISKS THAT MAY CAUSE SERIOUS INJURY OR WORSE. THESE RISKS INCLUDE FALLING ON ROCKS, TURNING AN ANKLE, BREAKING BONES AND GETTING LOST. ANYONE WHO PURCHASES THIS BOOK ASSUMES ALL RISK AND RESPONSIBILITY FOR HIS OR HER OWN SAFETY AND WELFARE.

The author has attempted to provide an accurate description for each route in this guidebook. However, a route listed in this book may or may not be safe for anyone to use at any given time. Routes vary in difficulty. The difficulty for hikers and trail runners will vary according to their experience, training and endurance. Trail conditions may change or deteriorate because of cataclysmic environmental or climactic events, new housing developments, logging, mining, wildfires, road-building or other circumstances beyond the author's control.

The trail descriptions and other information in this book are designed to help hikers and trail runners find new places to go and equip them with the necessary information about what to bring and how to prepare. Along with the information provided in this book, users may need to bring larger source maps for the areas they are recreating in to help with trail orientation. The travel times listed for a given hike or run are approximate. Actual travel time depends on a person's experience, endurance and conditioning.

Strenuous and epic trails listed in this book involve climbing on trails for a long period of time, which can lead to dehydration and exhaustion. Beginning hikers and runners should never attempt strenuous or epic trails until they have developed experience and endurance on shorter routes. Never embark on a hike or run late in the day – you could run out of time and get caught by darkness and freezing cold weather, perhaps leading to a nasty night spent out on the mountain without proper clothing or shelter.

Before you embark on a hike or a trail run, be sure to tell someone where you are going and leave them a map of the trail. If you get lost, call Ada County Mountain Search and Rescue at 911 or 846-7610. For other counties, call 911 or the sheriff's office for the county in which you are lost – Boise County, Owyhee County or Valley County.

Know your limitations and use common sense. It's better to give up on a hike or trail run than spend an uncomfortable night on the mountain. Be alert, watch for rocks and other obstacles and enjoy yourself.

Introduction

Late on a fall Sunday, I was running a long loop in Miltiary Reserve Park. I headed up Central Ridge Trail, popped out on the ridgetop, and felt a cool breeze against my cheeks. I zigzagged toward Shane's Loop on Bucktail, a really neat slalom-type trail, and then I climbed Shane's to the top, and took a moment to enjoy the pink and lavender glow in the sky.

It felt wonderful to be up there on Shane's Summit, knowing that the bulk of the climbing was over, and that this 7-mile run would burn plenty of calories. I looked forward to a hearty meal that evening with my sweetheart.

We are so fortunate to have a ton of hiking and running trails located so close to home in the Boise Valley – from the Greenbelt along the river, to the sweep of foothills between Eagle and Lucky Peak, and then more trails less than an hour's drive away in the Boise National Forest to the north and the Owyhee Mountains to the south.

I've been playing around on these trails for most of my adult life, hiking, mountain biking, running, snowshoeing and skiing. I was an avid peak-bagger, backpacker and road cyclist before mountain bikes were invented. When I had kids in my late 30s, the foothills trails that I knew like the back of my hand from cycling became a great place to take short hikes with kids in the backpack. Back in those days when I was tied to the house with two kids in diapers, a two-hour hike was a crucial break from the heavy-lifting at home. It helped to keep my sanity.

In the winter, when the trails are frozen or covered with a few inches of snow, I've often turned to trail running to stay in shape. You can get a great workout from an hour-long run in the foothills. This book project inspired me to do more trail running than ever before, and now I doubt I'll ever stop doing it, unless my knees or hips give out.

This book has been a significant challenge because I decided to include as many hiking and trail-running routes as possible, close to home. When I put together a list of routes within an hour's drive of Boise, it got pretty darn long, pretty darn quick – over 50. When I ground-proofed the list with experienced hikers and runners, it got even longer.

Well, we all like variety and diversity, so why not? I'd never thought of including routes in excess of a half-marathon until talking with folks in the running community who like to be challenged by runs even longer than that. So I created an epic category.

It's taken me years to cover all the trails described in this book. Every one of them contains something special. I hope you get out and explore each and every one of them. We are truly blessed to have so much access to public lands in every direction of the compass.

I also hope that the combination of hiking and running notes will encourage long-time hikers to consider doing a little trail running to see how you like it. And for the runners out there who rarely hike, take a moment to go for a stroll on the Greenbelt walking trail with your sweetheart and watch for bald eagles on a snowy January day. Or power-hike a national forest trail in the summer, and enjoy the wildflowers. The opportunities are nearly endless – just let your imagination go wild with the wind. - SS

Hiking and Running Tips

By Mike Carlson
Head Coach, BOISE Run/Walk
www.boiserunwalk.com

Want to start hiking or running on trails this year but aren't sure how best to get started? Like any new activity, you'll want to prepare your muscles, connective tissues, joints, and brain for the rigors you'll encounter along the way. Gravity, rocks, mud, uneven and sometimes loose footing, and other trail users are examples of challenges you should anticipate on the trail. As BOISE RunWalk's head coach, I want you to have fun and enjoy your experiences out there on the trails. I've been running for 37 years, won Race to Robie Creek 5 times, and competed in many other trail races, too. So with that experience, I've got some useful and important training tips for you.

Stretching before a hike/run should be a standard practice.

Once you've been given the go ahead by your doctor and chiropractor to begin your exercise program, you should first strengthen your legs and feet, and also your inner core to protect your spine. To achieve these goals, perform mixture of calisthenics, isometrics, plyometrics, and weight training. These exercises will help minimize or even eliminate any muscular weaknesses and imbalances between opposing muscle groups you might have. You should also improve your balance and agility through proprioceptive exercises to improve the communication between your central nervous system and your muscles. Flexibility is also important, so do plenty of stretching exercises. Any improvements you can make in your flexibility will allow your body to function and move more as it was designed to, thereby reducing the risk of injury and enhancing your ability to perform.

Once you're ready to get out onto the trails, start with short, not-too-challenging routes with small elevation gains, and then gradually increase the distance and intensity over several weeks. Don't forget to stay properly hydrated and nourished, and allow yourself to fully recover from your hard workouts before heading back to the trails again. Taking these steps will decrease the likelihood of injury and increase your enjoyment of the many wonderful trails in Southwest Idaho!

For more information contact Mike Carlson at 208-869-2089 or runmikecarlson@gmail.com.

Hiking and Running Tips (cont.)

Running shoes

For mountain hiking, I prefer to wear sturdy trail shoes with Vibram soles. They're pretty lightweight, but they've got a beefy heel support system for side-hilling control and hiking on rocks. Shoes like that will work just fine for any hikes in this book. That said, some folks may prefer wearing a beefier hiking boot on mountain trails. It's your call.

For trail running, many options exist for optimum foot wear. I recommend checking in with your favorite shoe store to explore the best fit, arch support and tread options.

Hydration

If you're hiking, carry at least a quart of water with you in a hydration pack, water bottle, whatever. I carry a Camelback Mule when I'm hiking. It's got plenty of room for an extra layer and shell, food, cell phone, keys, etc. If you're running less than an hour-long route, you may not need to pack water. For runs over an hour, the rule of thumb is to carry 5 to 10 ounces of liquid for every 15 minutes of running. Try out different water packs and waist-belt packs and find the one that's best in a running situation.

Etiquette/ethics

Aspire to be a great trail ambassador when you're out on the trail. Let people know when you're approaching by saying "coming up" or "on your left." Yield to uphill traffic on steep trails. Watch for people or bikes coming down the trail, and use your best judgment. Sometimes it's easiest for hikers or runners to step aside as bikes come up behind them or come down at them. On the other hand, I tell mountain bikers in my guidebooks to yield to uphill traffic, and to yield to hikers and runners whenever possible. So I think the key is to extend courtesy to other trail users, and they often will return the favor. If you run into a horse on the trail, it's good form to get off the trail and let horseback riders pass by. They typically travel faster than you. Talk to the riders as they approach so the horses won't spook.

The second thing is to know when to turn back when the trails are muddy. Don't be a bone-head and muck up the trails when they're wet and gooey. Just turn around and head for the Greenbelt or paved surfaces for your workout.

Dress in layers

In cool weather, it's important to dress for your workout in an intelligent way to increase comfort. Start with capeline garments – synthetic clothing that wicks away moisture as you perspire, and cap it off with running pants and an outer shell. When temperatures are in the 40s or below Fahrenheit, you may need a hat and gloves.

In the heat of the summer, watch out for sunburn and dehydration. A T-shirt will do in many conditions in the Boise Foothills and the Owyhee Mountains during the summer, but in the shoulder seasons, you can get stuck in a rainstorm or cold conditions. Anything goes at higher elevations in the Boise National Forest. Be sure to pack an extra layer and a shell in your Camelback for unforseen conditions. – SS

About public land agencies

The Ridge to Rivers Trail System

The Ridge to Rivers Trail System was established in 1992 when the Bureau of Land Management, Idaho Department of Lands, Ada County, Boise Parks & Recreation and the Boise National Forest agreed on a visionary multi-agency trail plan for the Boise Foothills. The vision was to create continuous trail corridors from the top of Bogus Basin Ski Resort to the Boise River Greenbelt, and it's a vision that worked.

The passage of the Boise Foothills $10 million levy in May 2000 created a much-needed public fund for purchasing key areas of open space, wildlife habitat and trails. Now there are more than 125 miles of trails in the Ridge to Rivers system, up from 80 in the 1990s.

Go to www.ridgetorivers.org, the Ridge to Rivers web site, for the latest trail conditions, dog leash policies and other updates.

You also may want to pick up a Ridge to Rivers trail map at your favorite outdoor store. The maps provide a big picture view of the trail system. This guidebook tells you the distance of the trails, how long it might take to hike or run them, and more.

Boise National Forest

Boise National Forest trails featured in this guidebook are located in the Idaho City Ranger District and the Emmett Ranger District. These are multiple-use trails open to hiking, biking and horseback riding, and sometimes, motorized uses as well.

Forest-wide maps are available in many locations, including the ranger district offices in Emmett or Idaho City, or at the Boise National Forest supervisor's office in Boise. Boise REI and map stores like Idaho Blueprint carry the maps as well. It's good to have an overview map of the Boise National Forest so you can best navigate the roads to the trailheads, and look for other trails you might enjoy.

To check on trail conditions, contact the Emmett Ranger District at 208-365-7000 or Idaho City Ranger District at 208-392-6681. The Emmett District has online information on trails: www.fs.fed.us/r4/boise/emmett/emmettrecreationindex.htm#Trails.

BLM

Trails in the Snake River canyon and in the Owyhee Mountains are managed by the Bureau of Land Management, Four Rivers District. Call 208-384-3300 for trail information at the Four Rivers District or 208-896-5912 at the Owyhee Field Office.

Idaho Department of Parks and Recreation

For information about trails and yurt rentals in the Idaho City Park 'n Ski area trail system, contact Idaho Parks at 208-334-4199 or www.parksandrecreation.idaho.gov.

Contacts for Greenbelt trails

Boise Parks and Recreation is the primary manager of the Boise River Greenbelt. See www.cityofboise.org/parks for information and updates or call 208-384-4240.

For information on the Eagle Greenbelt, call 208-489-8777. For information on the Nampa Greenbelt, call 468-5858. For information on the Caldwell Greenbelt, call 208-455-3060.

Dog doo is #1 issue on Foothills Trails
Follow dog-leash policies and pick up your dog's poop!

(Excerpted from the Boise Parks & Recreation Department web page)

An increase in dog waste is growing into a major problem in the Boise Foothills. More poop than ever is piling up at trailheads and along pathways, says David Gordon, Ridge to Rivers Trail Coordinator.

Make sure you pick up after Fido.

"Without question, the No. 1 negative comment that we receive is the amount of dog waste encountered on trails, followed closely by dogs off leash in on-leash areas," he says.

Dog owners frequently disregard on-leash trail restrictions in Hulls Gulch and Military Reserve. Foothills recreationists should check with the Parks Department on dog-leash areas; please follow the rules to avoid outright closures.

In 2003, an 11-member volunteer committee helped craft "controlled" off-leash regulations for dogs on selected trails. On controlled off-leash trails, dogs must remain within 30 feet of owners. Dogs are prohibited from approaching or harassing people, wildlife or other pets.

Off-leash trails comprise 95 percent of the Ridge to Rivers trail system. On-leash trails are located in the Camelsback/Lower Hulls Gulch area and Military Reserve.

Ridge to Rivers distributes 80,000 "mutt mitts" annually at a cost of $1,280.

Gordon estimates that the Ridge to Rivers crew picks up approximately 350 pounds of dog poop each week from trailhead trash cans. The biggest contributors are the Grove in Hulls Gulch, followed by the 9th Street Trailhead, Red Fox Trailhead and Military Reserve areas.

"When you look at what is provided for dog owners in terms of so many off-leash trails and all of the mutt mitt dispensers and trash cans, it really should be pretty simple to follow the rules," says Gordon. "Cities with similar trail systems have enacted stricter measures to gain compliance with dog owners. We may need to do that."

In recent years signage has been improved to educate dog owners about regulation. He also pointed out that Ridge to River's volunteer Trail Rangers spend a large portion of their time talking to dog owners about the rules, but the problem persists.

Boise Parks & Recreation held a public meeting in February 2008 about the issue. A citizens committee was charged with coming up with new solutions. Please visit the Ridge to Rivers web site, www.ridgetorivers.org, or www.cityofboise.org/Departments/Parks/Foothills, for more information.

Calendar of Events

January
Boise- **Bandanna's New Year's Day 5K Walk/Run**. Greg: 386-9017

February
Nampa- **Indoor Triathlon**: 1/2M Swim/10M Tetrix Bike/4M Run. Sherri Moro: 468-5777

March
Boise-**The Basic 5 St. Patrick's Day Run**. Bandanna: 386-9017
Boise-**Mad Hatter 5K Run or Walk**. josh@nostarclothing.com or 412-7234

April
Boise-**YMCA Spring Sprint Triathlon**: Swim–Run–Bike. Tim Severa: 344-5501
Ontario, OR-**Holy Gait 5K at Lions Park**: 541-881-7199
Boise-**Timberline Wolfpack Fun Run**: 5K Run. www.wolvesathletics.com
Boise-**Dry Creek Half Marathon Trail Run**: Jeff Ulmer: 888-2122
Boise-**Race to Robie Creek**: 13.1m. www.robiecreek.com

May
Caldwell-**YMCA Walk/Run for the Health of It**: 2.1m Run/Walk. Ineke: 455-3771
Boise-**The Hornet Run**: 5K Run/Walk. Kelly Cross or Jim Ashton: 250-4145
Boise-**Camelsback Duathlon**: Run–Bike–Run: 5K/30K/5K; 2K/8K/2K. Tim: 344-5501
Boise-**Race for the Cure**: 5K Run/Walk. komenboise@fiberpipe.com or 384-0013
Boise-**Hidden Springs Kids Run**: Jeff: 888-2122 or www.cityoftreesmarathon.com
Boise-**American Heart Walk**: 5K/1M Walks. American Heart Association: 384-5066
Boise-**Famous Idaho Potato Marathon**: 5K/10K/13.1m/26.2m. Tim Severa: 344-5501

June
Boise-**Ironman 70.3 Boise** 1.2M Swim/56M Bike/13.1M Run. www.ironmanboise.com
Boise-**St. Al's Capitol (Kids) Classic**: 2K Run.
Eagle-**Fireman's Fun Run**: 10K and a 1M kids Run. 939-6463
Boise-**YMCA Spudman Triathlon**: 1.5K Swim/40K Bike/10K Run. Tim: 344-5501
Meridian-**Meridian Dairy Days Milk Run**. 4K Run/Kid Run. 888-2817
Boise-**Roger Curran Memorial Run**. Sandi Francis: 921-8338.
Boise-**American Cancer Relay for Life**. Jenny Rapley: 422-0173
Caldwell-**Youth Tri-Classic** Swim/Bike/Run. John Downey: 459-4354
Meridian-**Barn Sour Run**: 888-3579
Boise-**Main Street Mile**: Greg at Bandanna: 386-9017

July
Melba-**Patriot Fun Run**: 6M Run, 2M Run/Walk. Lynn Perry: 495-2645
Boise-**JDRF Walk To Cure Diabetes**: 3K Walk. Beth: 336-2703
Nampa-**Stampede Through Town**: 5K Run/Walk/10K Run. Carol: 466-4641, ext. 105
Boise-**Fit for Life**: 13.1M/ 10K/5K. Jeff Ulmer 888-2122 www.cityoftreesmarathon.com

August
Boise-**Foothills XC 12K Trail Race**: Idaho Nordic: Spondoro.com
Kuna-**Kuna Days 5K**: Jeff Ulmer 888-2122 or www.cityoftreesmarathon.com
Boise-**Y-Not-Tri Triathlon**: 1/4M Swim–6M Bike–2M Run. Tim Severa: 344-5501
Ontario, OR-**A Fair Run 5K & 10K**: fit4life@cableone.net or Kent: 541-889-8877
Emmett-**Emmett Most Excellent Triathlon**: www.boiseaeros.com

September

Boise-**Hidden Springs School Daze Fun Run**: 1M kids race. Jeff Ulmer 888-2122

Boise-**Table Rock Challenge**: 9M Run/Walk. Kelly Woods: 373-4261

Boise-**Run With the Animals**: 5K Run/Walk. www.spondoro.com

Boise-**YMCA Hidden Springs Duathlon**: 4/5M Run/5/10M Bike. Tim: 344-5501

Caldwell-**Kiwanis Indian Creek Run/Walk**: 10K Run, 5K Run/Walk. Dave: 459-4574

Boise-**St. Luke's Women's Fitness Celebration**. 5K Run/Walk. Melissa: 381-2221

Eagle-**Bob Firman Cross Country Open**: 5K. Gregg at Bandanna: 386-9017

Boise-**See Spot Walk**: 1M/3M Walk. Christine Moore: 342-3508, ext. 231

October

Nampa-**Harvest Classic**: 2M/8K Run/Walk/WC, 1M Kids. Wendy: 468-5858

Nampa-**Beginners Triathlon**: 1/8M Swim–4M Tetrix Bike–1.5M Run. Sherri: 468-5777

The St. Luke's Women's Fitness Celebration 5K run/walk is a huge Boise event. (Photo courtesy the St. Luke's Women's Fitness Celebration)

Boise-**City of Trees Kids Marathon**: 1.2M. Ruth Ulmer: 888-2122

Boise-**Harrison Kids Classic**: 1M. Tim Severa: 344-5501

Caldwell-**Canyon County Kids Classic**: 1M. Tim Severa: 344-5501

Meridian-**Meridian Kids** Classic: 1M. Tim Severa: 344-5501

Boise-**Barber to Boise**: 6.2M Run/Walk. 5K Run/Walk. Tim Severa: 344-5501

Eagle-**Eagle Treasure Valley Pumpkin Race**: 1M/5K. Ed Schonberger: 371-2344

Caldwell-**Monster Dash 2007**: 1M Kids Run, 5K Run/Walk. Brian Faulks: 455-8000

Boise-**Prison Break Half Marathon**: 10K/5K. www.prisonbreakhalf.com

Boise-**Brew Pub Volksmarch**. Juliann Fritchman: 345-8259

November

Garden City-**Zeitgeist Half Marathon**. 853-1221 or zhalfmarathon.com

Boise-**Catch Me If You Can 5K Run/Walk**. Greg Morris: 493-2503

Boise-**Veterans Day Kids Run**: 1.2M/5K. Jeff Ulmer: 888-2122

Boise-**Turkey Trot Relay**: 4x2M. Diane McGarvey: 345-9947

December

Boise-**Christmas Walk**. Juliann Fritchman: 345-8259

Boise-**YMCA Christmas Run**: 2.5M Run/Walk, 6.1M Run. Tim Severa: 344-5501

Photo Gallery

The backbone of the Bruneau Sand Dunes rises up 500 feet above the Snake River Valley, providing fetching views of the surrounding area. Plus, it's a great launching pad for playing in the sand.

Red Fox Trail near Camelsback Park winds by the Hulls Ponds area before venturing into the foothills. It's a popular trail for hiking, running and biking.

It's always fun to run into friends on the trail. Here, we're checking out the new trails in Polecat Gulch on a fall day in the NW Foothills.

Jump Creek Canyon, near Marsing, is a scenic place to visit with the family. The hike to the waterfall is only 1/4-mile long. The waterfall flows year-round.

The Boise Bs cruise up the Corrals Trail, a popular moderate hike/run in Boise's Central Foothills . It's a great loop to take Corrals over Corrals Summit to Bob's Trail or Camelsback Park.

This is what it's all about when the kids are young and fit into a backpack. Here's Steve hiking in Orchard Gulch when son Quinn was about 8 months old.

Spring hiking in the Owyhees is always a treat, especially in the sunshine. Bring your flower book and binoculars when you go out there in the spring. Watch for deer, antelope and hawks.

Dave Williams

*It's easy to climb above Blue Lake near Snowbank Mountain
and catch the big view of Long Valley and the mountains beyond.*

*The Elkhorn Yurt in the Idaho City Park 'n Ski Trail system is well-
positioned for maximum views. This is a great place to go hiking or trail
running, and then stay in a yurt and party with friends at night.*

*Early Native American
tribes in the Snake River
area inscribed many large
boulders near Celebration
Park with unique drawings,
known as petroglpyhs. It's
all part of the experience
when you go hiking or
running to Halverson Lake.*

Race to Robie Creek
The toughest half-marathon in the Northwest

In 1975, Jon Robertson invited 25 friends on a hot August night's fun run up Rocky Canyon to Robie Creek near Boise, Idaho. The winding, sand-gravel route through sagebrush-covered hills – the old stagecoach road to Idaho City during the gold rush of the 1860s – measured about 13 miles, an eight-mile climb to 4,797-foot Aldape Summit and a steep, five-mile descent. When Robertson was a kid, he panned for gold in the area with his father.

Today, the "Race to Robie Creek," a grueling half-marathon promoted as one of the toughest races in the Northwest, is a 23-year-old rite of spring, a test of stamina for

Courtesy Race to Robie Creek

Homing pigeons are released at the start of the Race to Robie Creek. Every year, there's a new theme at the start. None of them are conventional.

about 3,000 walkers and runners, an excuse for a big party, and an important source of revenue for charities benefitting children, families, ethnic groups, and even wildlife.

Early in January, local runners and walkers look toward the third week in April and ask each other: "Are you doing Robie?" The answer is usually preceded by a groan, then a sigh, and finally a grudging smile. "I think it's the toughest long race in the Northwest with as many people participating, the rough terrain, and the need for good, logistical support," Robertson says. "If you train for it seriously, it's as difficult as a marathon on the flat."

Jack Kaper, a retired social worker in Boise, has been involved in organizing Robie since its third year. A miler in high school, he has run the race more than a dozen times, his personal best was one hour, 39 minutes.

The vision in the 1970s was to have a demanding race with a free party at the end for participants, their families and friends. By Robie IV, organizers decided to add a little spice to the race start ceremonies.

Kaper remembers, "Glen Woods, our 1962 state discus champion, threw a discus in the air, and when it landed in the middle of the road, 80 feet in front of the runners, the race began."

What's unusual about that? The composition of the discus for one thing, fashioned from flour and the ground-up remains of toads found in Rocky Canyon on the road to Robie Creek, so flattened by passing motor vehicles they could be picked up and sailed frisbee-like through the air. And so the Rocky Canyon Sail Toads, the group which produced the race, started a grand tradition.

The Robie logo, an uncrossed "A" that many racers think is a fair representation of the tough course, is a Japanese slash created by Boise painter/runner Nunzio Lagattuta. Many of the poster and T-shirt versions year after year are produced by Sally Stevens, a professional graphic artist and designer who operates a business called Idea-Monger. She also is president and co-owner of the new coffee shop on Broadway.

Sail Toad Kaper is still in charge of fun starts. "We begin at the Boise Community Center, then make a long loop before heading uphill. We try to generate an energy so walkers and runners make that first loop with smiles on their faces."

Over the years, unique and entertaining starts – always closely-guarded secrets – have featured an exploding, feather-filled balloon, Native Americans dancing in a drum circle, a 300-pound Samoan jumping on a flip board to launch a coconut, Jell-O-filled papier-mâché toads dropped from a high platform, a wedding, and a giant Hollywood director's scene-take board cracking the beginning of "The Race to Robie Creek – The Movie."

Phil McClain

Watch out for ruts on Rocky Canyon Road. Some years are worse than others. But the granite soil scours easily.

Kaper's favorite? "The year we had parachutists. One guy jumped from 7,000 feet and landed with both feet on the target zone. That got the crowd energized!"

One of the wildest was the start in 1992. The theme "Wild Thing!" was carried out by the rumbling entrance of Boise's motorcycle gang, Brother Speed – nine bikers riding classic Harleys to the blaring sounds of Steppenwolf's 1960s hit, "Born to Be Wild."

A specially-assembled rock group, "The Croakettes," including Stevens, race director that year, entertained the crowd with an inspired rendition of the Troggs' hit, "Wild Thing!" A vintage pink Cadillac delivered the leather-and-leopard-attired singers to the stage. Some walkers and runners went the distance in costume, including bunny visors and odd-shaped sunglasses.

Following the races, the fun continues at the Robie Creek Picnic Area for participants, families and friends, with distribution of purple T-shirts, a catered picnic for 6,000 with hot dogs, Idaho potatoes, special beer, and a ceremony with awards and fun gifts. Prizes in the past have included trips, dinners, and $100 bills to vasectomies and divorces.

While the "Race to Robie Creek" is meant to be fun, there is a serious side to the proceedings. Thousands of dollars are collected from entry fees and contributions by local businesses and corporations.

Charities that the race supported in recent years include: the Native American Coalition, Basque Charities, Mountain Search & Rescue, YMCA, Idaho Food Bank, Robie Creek Volunteer Fire Department, Meals on Wheels, Hannabou Moroccan Road Race, Mores Creek Ambulance, Madison Head Start, Special Olympics Idaho, Foster Care Fund and many more are previous recipients of race donations. Last year the race donated more than $57,000 to the various charities!

Major Race Sponsors include: Bandanna Running and Walking, AceCo., Nagel Beverage/Pepsi, Shu's Idaho Running Company, Highlands Hollow, Centennial Job Corps, Simplot Food Group, Idaho Department of Parks and Rec., The Idaho Statesman, Tates Rents, Budweiser, Sysco Food Services and URS Washington Division. We couldn't do it without them!

Kaper continues to think about unusual starts for the "Race to Robie Creek," including the 100th running. "We won't be here, of course, but the original Sail Toads have discussed one idea. We could be cremated and our ashes spread on the ground for the starting line. What do you think?" First Sail Toad Robertson is amused but will not participate. "My body fluids and other essences are all over that course. I have already contributed body molecules to every square inch. I'll take my chances with Morris Hill Cemetery!"

"This race has always been known as fun and open. I remember how we cheered when entries reached 100, 500, then 1,000. We didn't think it would get this big (now nearly 2,400)," he said.

Training tips for Race to Robie Creek

By Mike Carlson, Head Coach, BOISE Run/Walk

1. The 13.1 mile course climbs 2,100 feet over the first 8.6 miles to Aldape Summit and descends 1,700 feet over the remaining 4.5 miles.
2. The surfaces are pavement for the first 3.4 miles and a dirt/gravel road for the remainder. While running on any surface, but especially in the hills, watch where you put your feet. In heavy snow years, you might find snow and/or mud spots on Aldape Summit on race day, especially during the first mile of descent.
3. The best way to prepare for any event is to simulate in training what you'll be doing on race day. So if you're training for Robie Creek that means you must train on hills. And what better hills to train on than those on the race course!
4. Run long in the hills once a week if you're accustomed to running hills, or once every other week if you aren't.
5. Practice good up and downhill running form. Run vertically (no forward lean) uphill and run perpendicularly to the grade on the downhill (slight full-body lean). Take three steps per second to maximize efficiency and minimize the pounding.
6. Strengthen your inner core, leg muscles and tendons to improve your balance.
7. In April, the weather can vary greatly, but it's typically fairly warm and often humid. Train in warm conditions—indoors or during the warmest part of the day—to prepare.
8. Good shoes and insoles will serve you well on the descent from Aldape Summit. Make sure your shoes and insoles aren't worn out, but are broken in.

Mike Carlson

By Andrija Barker-McCurry, Bandanna Running and Walking

1. Don't ignore the downhills. Everyone trains for the climb but it seems no one trains for the downhill aspect of Robie Creek. The uphill works your engine, but it is the downhill that beats up your body.
2. Don't get too technical, thinking you should only train on the course or similar terrain. Boost your maximum oxygen uptake by throwing in interval work. Example: Run 200 meter repeats on your local track. 200 meters moderate to hard followed by 200 meters walk or jog recovery. Also, hill repeats. Run uphill hard for 30-60 seconds, turn around and jog down.

Andrija Barker-McCurry

Training tips for Race to Robie Creek

3. Remember nutrition. It is not what you eat the night before, or even the morning of – the weeks leading up to the race are the ones that count.
4. Recognize that Robie is not your local nine o'clock 5k. It is vital to eat enough the morning of to correctly fuel your effort. My favorite is a hearty bowl of oatmeal, a banana, a small glass of juice and a piece of toast. Eat three hours before the race and then have a small snack or a GU fifteen to twenty minutes before race time.
5. Nutrition during the race can be confusing. Glycogen depletion usually begins to take affect when you run over ninety minutes. So, plan on taking a GU or the like and a small amount of liquid if you are running over 90 minutes. If you're out there over two hours, plan on at least two GU's plus liquid.

By the late Erv Olen, 65, who ran the Race to Robie Creek 22 times

1. Start at least four months before the race (January 1st).
2. Run hills one day every other week. Start with 6 miles (3 up, 3 down), and work up to 12+ miles. I suggest running on the Robie Creek course.
3. Gradually increase weekly long runs to16 miles.
4. Include weekly speed work. Alternate the following workouts: Start with 4 each 400 meters on a track at 5K pace with 200 meter slow jog in between. Build up to 6 each 1/2 mile intervals at 5K pace. Do hill sprints about 300 meters each. Start with 4 and work up to 8. Let heart rate get down to 100 beats per minute before repeating.

Erv Olen

5. Every other week, do tempo runs. Start with 3-4 miles, work up to 6-8 miles. Run pace should be 15 seconds per mile slower than 10K pace.
6. Stretch well before and after workouts. Do easy runs in between hard days. It helps to do weight work 2 or 3 days a week. One rest day a week is a good thing. This schedule will get you ready for Robie Creek. Be sure to taper 2 weeks before race. (*My friend Erv was struck with cancer as he was training for his 23rd Robie in spring 2008; he died in May 2008*).

By Maggie Lawrence, a frequent Race to Robie Creek participant

1. When training on Rocky Canyon Road, I recommend for the longer runs (8-10 miles), running a shuttle part way up the hill so you don't have to run all the downhill on your way back.
2. For safety reasons, I don't recommend running solo on weekdays in Rocky Canyon; however, on weekends in March and April, there are many other runners out there.
3. I run the summit two weeks before the race.

Maggie Lawrence

Running and Hiking Clubs/Groups
How to hook up ...

• **Boise Women's Hiking Network Yahoo Group (Boise WHN)** - A group for women of all ages in the Boise metropolitan area who enjoy hiking, backpacking, snowshoeing, skiing and other outdoor sports. Any member can invite others on an outing by posting her hiking plans to the group. Activities include day hikes, coed and women-only camping and backpacking trips, monthly potlucks, and any other trips that members wish to plan. Go to Yahoo Groups: groups.yahoo.com/group/BoiseWHN/.

• **Idaho Outdoors Yahoo Group** - A place where people can post questions or invitations to Boise-area outdoorsy types who are game for hiking, biking, climbing, weekend outings - you name it. Go to Yahoo Groups: groups.yahoo.com/group/idahooutdoors.

• **Idaho Mountain Recreation Club** - A new club founded in Boise in January, 2007. More than an outings club, IMR focuses on outdoor activities and in helping people enjoy the outdoors safely and responsibly. Enjoy a wealth of regularly scheduled trips and training classes. Count on a group of friends with similiar experience levels to join you in the outdoors. Go to idahomountainrec.org.

• **Boise Run/Walk** - Walkers, runners, coach Potatoes, too! Get in the best shape of your life and have fun! It's never too late to join. Boise Run/Walk is an organization that provides regular group run/walk outings for people training for upcoming race events or just trying to get off the couch. Go to: www.boiserunwalk.com.

• **The Y Striders Running Club** - The Y-Striders is a non-profit organization whose goal is to make Boise a better place to live and run through promotion and support of local running events. The Club meets regularly for weekly runs and provides advice, support and great training opportunities. Go to www.boiseystriders.org.

• **Hash House Harriers** - Drinking. Running. That's all. The Harriers are really more of a drinking club with a running problem. The group meets once a week on Monday nights for exercise and fun. If you are new to Boise, or like to drink beer, run or if you crave acceptance from a group of not-too-discriminating people, feel free to join us. Go to www.boiseh3.org.

• **The Boise Aggies** - The Boise Aggies are local members of the Northern California running club, the Asics Aggies. Their goal is to provide an opportunity for runners of all abilities to train together with a group of local runners. The group includes a wide range of talent, from national-class masters (40+ age group), Olympic Trials hopefuls, triathletes, and recreational runners aspiring to go to the next level. Go to www.boiseaggies.com.

• **Bandanna Running and Walking** - 504 W. Main St., Downtown Boise, 386-9017. Check for weekly outings at www.bandannarunning.com.

• **Shu's Idaho Running Company** - 1758 W. State St., Albertson's Marketplace, 344-6604. Check for weekly outings at www.idahorunningcompany.com.

About the Rating System

A quick glance at the Table of Contents (Pages 3-4) may have given you a sense for how I organized the 75 routes in the book. I created five general categories:

☐ **Greenbelt Trails** - These trails are essentially flat with a few dips and inclines here and there. Vertical gain is less than 10 feet per mile.

☐ **Easy Mountain Trails** - Trails that are generally pretty short distance-wise, and fairly flat in mountain terms. But they still may feature 500 vertical feet of climbing over several miles.

☐ **Moderate Mountain Trails** - These trails are longer than easy trails, and they take longer to complete, but the climbing isn't too bad gradient-wise, and the overall climbs are typically less than 1,500 feet.

☐ **Strenuous Mountain Trails** - Trails that will make your heart pound and your body hurt, at least during the climbing phase of the route. These trails are for the more advanced hiker/runner who enjoys being challenged by distance, steep vertical climbing, and time on the trail.

☐ **Epic Mountain Trails** - These trails are especially guaranteed to kick butt. The routes are longer than 10 miles, and the vertical gain may exceed 3,000 feet. A full day will be required for epic hikes, and more than 3 hours for some of the runs. Don't try these first.

For each trail description, the following key terms are defined:

Location: The geographic location of the hike/run in general terms.

Difficulty: How the hike/run rates according to the terms listed above. Even some easy hikes/runs may have a strenuous pitch or two, but overall, they are easy compared to moderate or strenuous routes.

Distance: The length of the route in miles.

Tread: What type of trail tread you'll be hiking/running on, whether it's a dirt road, 4WD dirt road or two-track roads (more narrow with ruts), paved trail (greenbelt) or singletrack (a single dirt path).

Hiking time: The time it would take an average person to hike the route, based on how long it took me or the person logging the route. Sometimes these times are listed in a range, between how fast a power hiker might finish the route, versus a person who is on a pleasure walk.

Running time: The time it took to run a route either by the person logging it or me. I run pretty slow (10K or 6 miles in about an hour on mountain trails). So gauge how fast you might finish a trail based on how long it takes you to run other courses of the same distance.

Vertical gain: How many vertical feet of gain and loss from start to finish.

Water: This refers to the availability of water along the trail for dogs.

Watch out for: Hazards that you may encounter along the trail.

Season: Time of year when the trail is best-suited for public use.

Map Legend

——————— Trail Route

- - - - - - - Optional Route

(S/F) Start/Finish

(S) Start

(F) Finish

(21) State Highway

(84) Interstate Highway

535 USFS road

⇒ Direction of travel

2,740' Elevation above sea level

P Parking area

Public Rest Room

Greenbelt Trails

1. Eagle Greenbelt to Riverside Park (p. 28)
2. Veterans Park to Glenwood (p. 30)
3. Veterans Park - Garden City Loop (p. 32)
4. Veterans Park Pond Loop (p. 34)
5. Greenbelt Underpass Special (p. 36)
6. Capital to ParkCenter Loop (p. 38)
7. Municipal Park to Barber Park Loop (p. 40)
8. Barber Park to River Run walking path (p. 42)
9. Kathryn Albertsons Park Loop (p. 44)
10. Eckert Road to Lucky Peak (p. 46)
11. Nampa Greenbelt (p. 48)
12. Caldwell Greenbelt (p. 50)

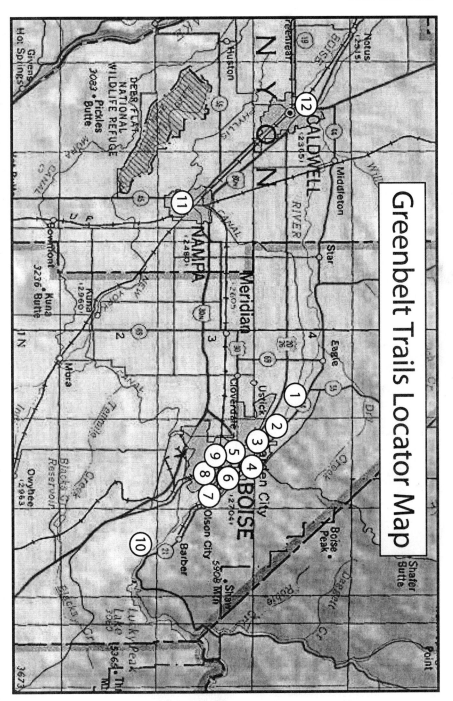

Greenbelt Trails Locator Map

#I Eagle Greenbelt to Riverside Park

Location: Eagle Road - ID 44
Difficulty: Easy to moderate
Distance: 4.6 miles
Tread: Paved, dirt greenbelt
Hiking time: 2 hours
Running time: 55 minutes
Vertical gain: 55 feet
Watch out for: Wildlife, other greenbelt users
Water: Dependable in Boise River
Season: Year-round

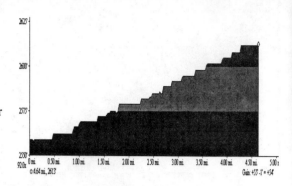

Getting there: In downtown Boise, take W. State Street about eight miles to Eagle Road. Turn left, and then take another left into Eagle River. Follow signs on the right to the Hilton Inn and Bardenay. The hike/run starts here. **Shuttle**: Leave a vehicle in the public parking lot on the south side of the Boise River bridge on Glenwood Avenue.

General notes: It's exciting that it's possible to piece together a route that connects between the Eagle Greenbelt and the Riverside Village Greenbelt. The route is slightly uphill the whole way, but only 55 feet over 4.6 miles. The middle section of the trail zigzags through a subdivision before connecting to the Riverside Village walking path. It's dirt most of the way. There are many places where you could pull off the trail to have a picnic or go fishing.

Directions: Head toward the Boise River and pick up the paved Greenbelt trail behind Bardenay. Go left and cruise along the river. More than 2.5 miles east of the start, the trail enters a subdivision with gated sections. Follow the signs and the bike/foot tracks to stay with the trail. Then you enter the Riverside Village Greenbelt at mile 3.3. You'll wind along a seam between the river and the exclusive development for another 1.3 miles to finish at 4.6. Cross the Glenwood Bridge and go left at the traffic light to reach the Glenwood greenbelt parking lot.

The Hike: Take your time and enjoy it. Bring some drinks and snacks and take in the scenery. Watch for herons, kingfishers, waterfowl, bald eagles and more. Mosquitoes can be an issue in the early summer.

The Run: The Eagle Greenbelt and Riverside Village Greenbelt offer a scenic and varied experience along the Boise River. There's nice footing on a dirt wood-chip trail. Arrange for a dropoff or pickup at Glenwood, or do the shuttle. Strong runners may want to go out and back for a 9.2-mile jaunt. – SS

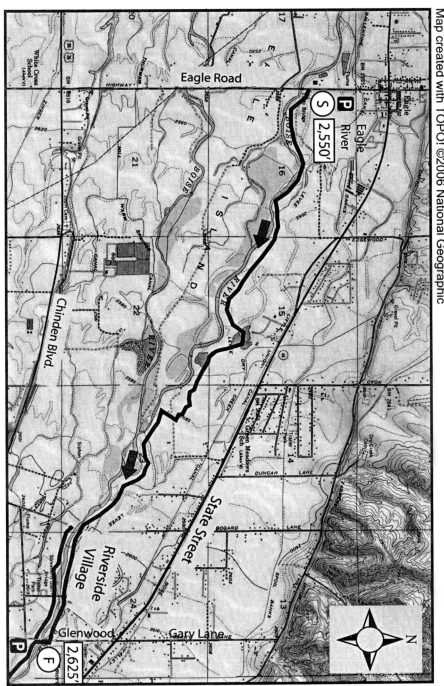

#2 Veterans Park to Glenwood

Location: Boise River Greenbelt,
Veterans Park
Difficulty: Easy
Distance: 3.75 miles
Tread: Paved greenbelt path
Hiking time: 1+ hours
Running time: 30 minutes or less
Vertical loss: 50 feet
Watch out for: Wildlife, other
greenbelt users
Water: Dependable in Boise River
Season: Year-round

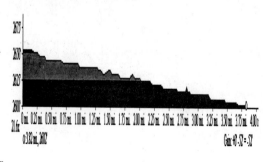

Getting there: In downtown Boise, take W. State Street to the traffic light at 36th Street and Veterans Parkway. Go left on Veterans Parkway and then turn left into Veterans State Park. The hike/run starts here. **Shuttle**: Plant a vehicle at the greenbelt-Glenwood Bridge parking lot or arrange for pickup or dropoff by a friend or family member.

General notes: The greenbelt doesn't run on both sides of the river in this reach, so this Greenbelt section is best traveled as a shuttle or out and back. It is a scenic section of the Greenbelt, running through a leafy section next to Willow Lane Park, a woodsy section between Willow Lane and Lake Harbor, and more leafy sections between Lake Harbor. There are cool bridges that cross islands in the Boise River before the final approach to Glenwood next to the Les Bois horse stables. You can lengthen the hike/run by continuing on the greenbelt west of Glenwood for a little over a mile before it ends.

Directions: Start the hike/run from either the main Veterans Park area, where there are rest rooms, or the parking area in the southwest side of the park (more direct). Go across the walking bridge over the canal, and then bear right and head over to the main greenbelt path. You'll cross another canal on a new bridge. Turn right on the main greenbelt. Bear left and follow the pathway under Veterans Parkway Bridge and then stay on the pathway through Willow Lane, Lake Harbor and then cross the steel bridges over the pathway next to Les Bois Park. The path runs for about a mile now to Glenwood Bridge.

The Hike: Take your time and enjoy it.

The Run: This is a perfect route for folks who like to run about 3 to 5 miles. The pathway on the north side of the river by Glenwood goes all the way to Eagle if you'd like to add 4.5 miles to your workout. – SS

Map created with TOPO! ©2006 National Geographic

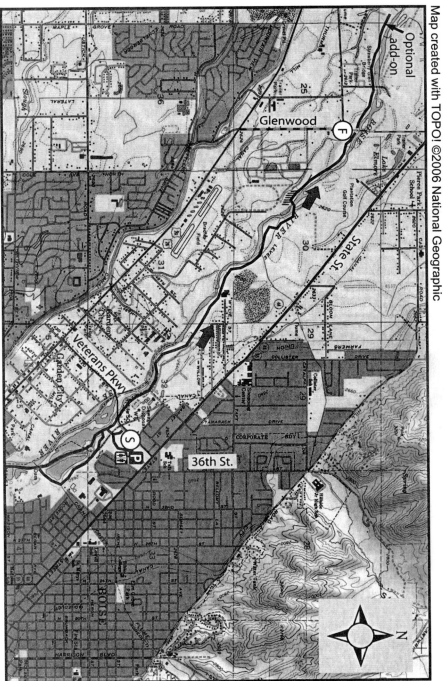

#3 Veterans Park - Garden City Loop

Location: Boise River Greenbelt
Difficulty: Easy
Distance: 3.25 miles
Tread: Paved, dirt greenbelt
Hiking time: 1+ hours
Running time: 30 minutes or less
Vertical gain: 25 feet
Watch out for: Wildlife, other greenbelt users
Water: Dependable in Boise River
Season: Year-round

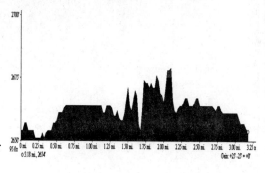

Getting there: In downtown Boise, take W. State Street to the traffic light at 36th Street and Veterans Parkway. Go left on Veterans Parkway and then turn left into Veterans State Park. The hike/run starts here.

General notes: This is a nifty lunchtime or after-work running route, and it's a great hiking loop anytime you've got an hour or so to spare. The loop is scenic because you cruise by several rapids on the Boise River, including an old diversion dam that attracts play-boaters, and there are lots of ducks and geese that frequent the Veterans Park ponds. Thanks to Garden City for getting more of the Greenbelt completed on the south side of the river. It's great to have these new Greenbelt loops where you can travel on both sides of the river. Enjoy!

Directions: Start the hike/run from either the main Veterans Park area, where there are rest rooms, or the parking area in the southwest side of the park (more direct). Go across the walking bridge over the canal, and then bear right and head over to the main greenbelt path. You'll cross another canal on a new bridge. Turn right on the main greenbelt. Head up the path to the Veterans Parkway Bridge (don't take the underpass), go left on the bridge sidewalk, and then go left again to jump onto the Garden City Greenbelt. Now it's clear sailing for about 1.5 miles on the pathway to the Main Street Bridge. Peel off the path at the bridge and go up on the bridge sidewalk, turn left, cross the river, then turn left again to head back to Veterans Park. You'll pass by Quinn's Pond (best place for swimming), and then cross a wooden bridge next to a rapids and enter the Veterans Park area. After you cross the bridge, bear right to take the dirt path around the north side of the Veterans Park ponds (either the paved or dirt path works) and return to the trailhead.

The Hike: Take your time and enjoy it. Bring some drinks and snacks.

The Run: This is a perfect route for folks who like to run about 3 miles. Take a second lap around the Veterans Park ponds if you still have the energy. – SS

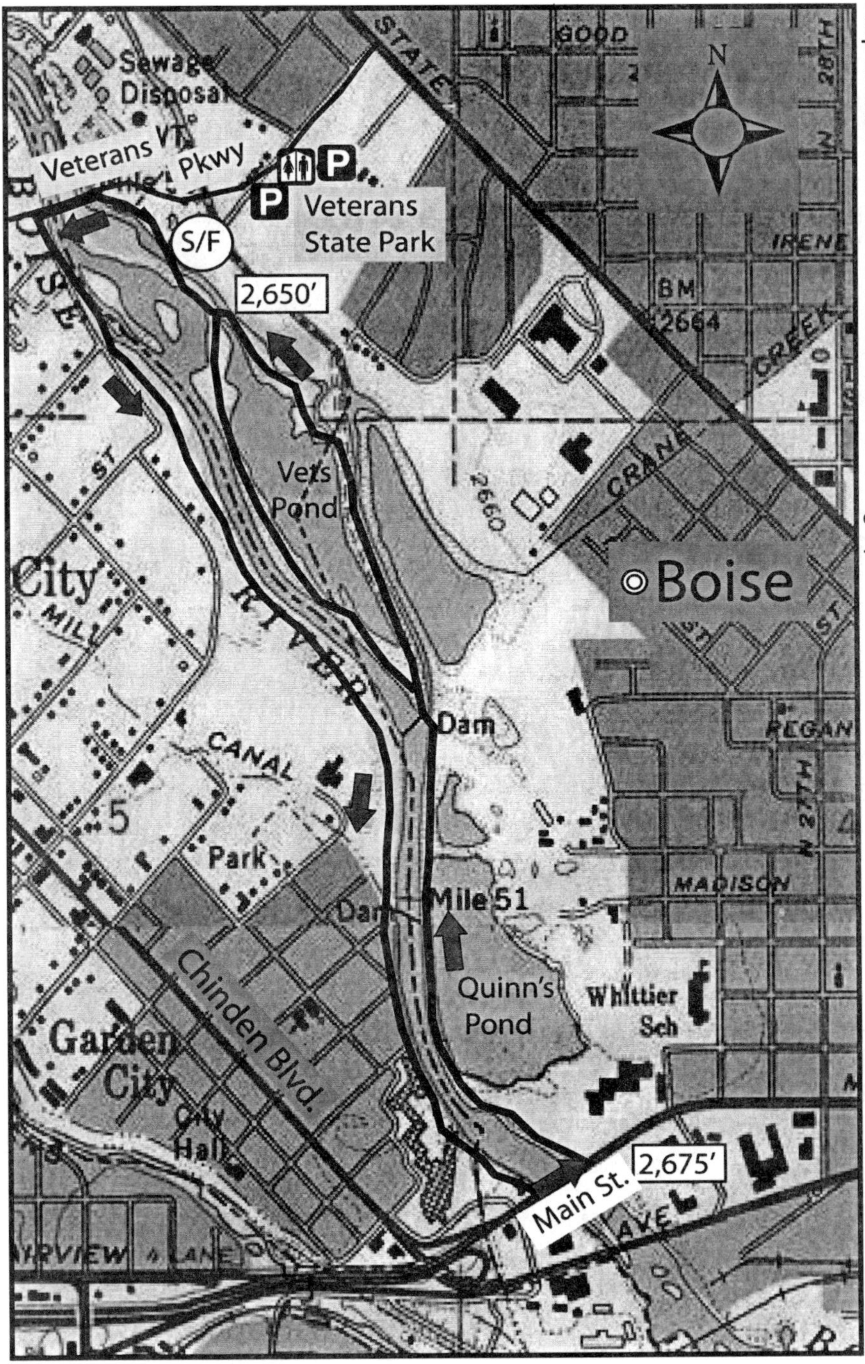

N

Sewage Disposal

Veterans VT
Veterans Pkwy

P 🚻 P
Veterans
State Park

S/F

2,650'

Vets
Pond

28TH

GOOD

IRENE

BM
2664

CRANE

CREEK

City

MILL

ST

RIVER

2660

©Boise

N 27TH

REGAN

Dam

CANAL

5

Park

Dam

Mile 51

MADISON

Quinn's
Pond

Whittier
Sch

Garden
City

Chinden Blvd.

City
Hall

Main St. 2,675'

FAIRVIEW 4 LANE

AVE

#4 Veterans Park Pond Loop

Location: Veterans Park in Boise
Difficulty: Easy
Distance: 1.6 miles
Tread: Dirt and paved greenbelt
Hiking time: 45 minutes - 1 hour
(leisurely pace)
Running time: 20 minutes
Vertical gain: 5 feet
Watch out for: Wildlife, other
greenbelt users
Water: Dependable in Boise River
and Veterans Park ponds
Season: Year-round

Getting there: From downtown Boise, take west State Street to the junction of 36th Street and Veterans Parkway. Turn left at the traffic light on Veterans Parkway, and then turn left into the park. The hike/run starts here. You can park in the central area of the park near rest rooms, or in the southwest portion of the park for more direct access to the Greenbelt.

General notes: The loop around Veterans Park Pond is a low-key hike/run in a scenic area of the greenbelt where you can take the dirt path around the pond, and then loop back on the paved greenbelt to Veterans State Park. This is a great little loop for bird-watching next to the ponds and the river. It's also a perfect short hike for kids, where they can play next to the ponds, skip rocks or do a little fishing. And it's a short run for those who like to keep mileage under 2 miles.

Directions: From the center of Veterans Park, take one of several paths that head south toward the river. Cross the canal bridge and bear left to head for the dirt pathway around Veterans pond. Follow the trail next to the pond. It's about .8 miles to the point where the dirt trail merges with the paved greenbelt by a small rapids in the river. Turn right and take the greenbelt west for a half-mile to a bridge over the canal and return to the central area of the park where you started. If you reach the Veterans Parkway bridge, you missed the turn to return to the park. Feel free to check out more areas of the Greenbelt, as you have time and energy. The path going west toward Willow Lane Park is quite scenic and enjoyable as well.

The Hike: This is often a nice, quiet area along Veterans Park Pond, especially during the week. On weekends and summer evenings, it can get more busy and crowded.

The Run: This is an easy short run around the pond. If you want to increase mileage, do the loop and then run it in reverse to bring mileage to 3.2. – SS

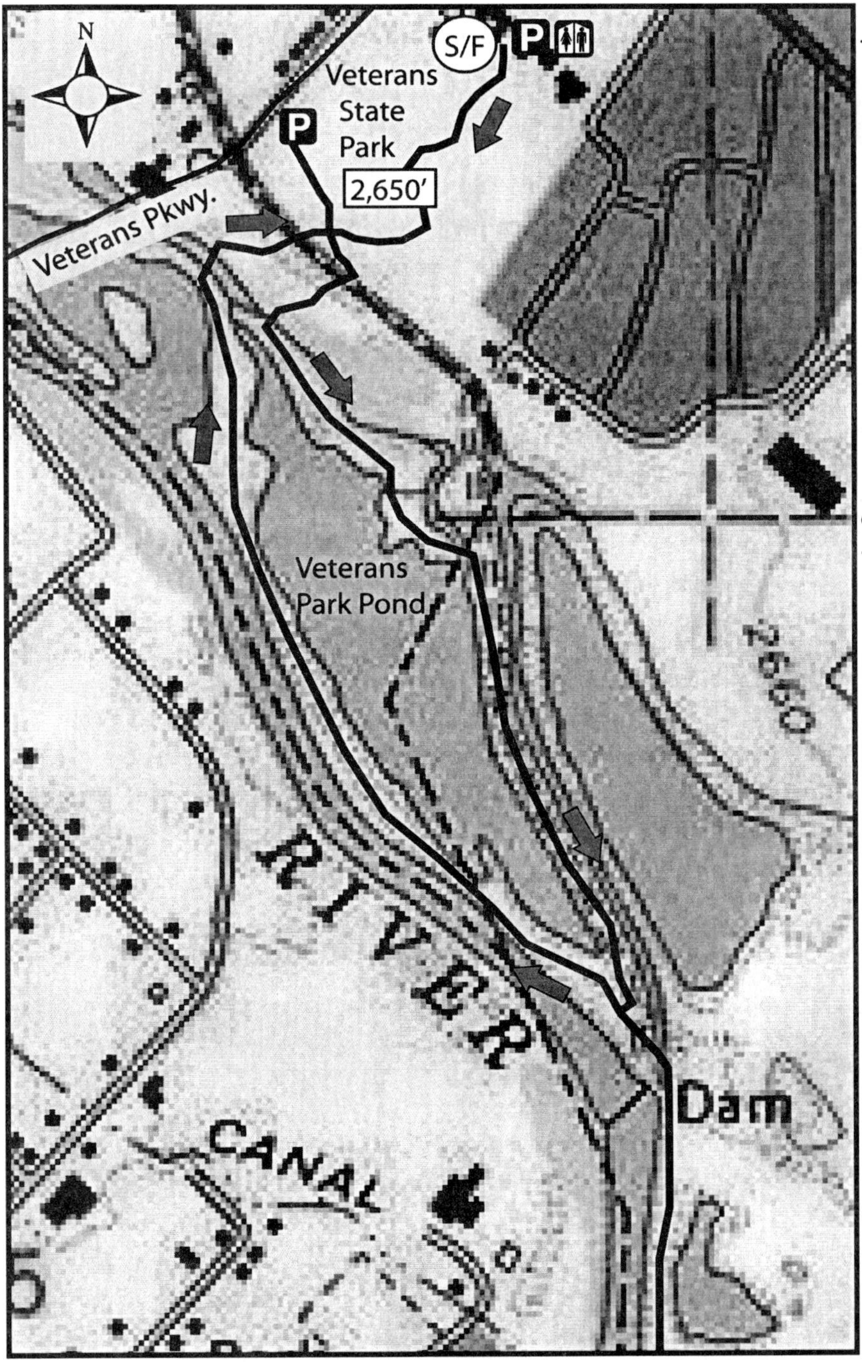

N

P

S/F P 🚻

Veterans
State
Park

2,650'

Veterans Pkwy.

Veterans
Park Pond

R I V E R

2660

Dam

CANAL

Map created with TOPO! ©2006 National Geographic

#5 Greenbelt Underpass Special

Location: Boise River Greenbelt
Difficulty: Moderate
Distance: 4.3 miles
Tread: Paved greenbelt
Hiking time: 1:30
Running time: 40 minutes
Vertical gain: 30 feet
Watch out for: Wildlife, other greenbelt users
Water: Dependable in Boise River
Season: Year-round

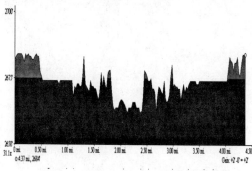

Getting there: In downtown Boise, take 9th Street south to River Street. Turn left on River and follow it over to Capital. Go across Capital on River and enter Julia Davis Park. Turn right and find a place to park along the greenbelt. Walk over to the junction of the greenbelt and the Capital Bridge. This is Mile 0. The hike/run starts here.

General notes: This is a nifty lunchtime running route for folks who work downtown, and it's a nice hike, too. The route runs west along a greenbelt parkway underneath six – count 'em six – bridges, creating opportunities to scream and echo (my kids love to do that) or not. You'll cruise by Quinn's Pond, a great summertime swimming hole, and then turn around at the 2.0 mile mark, at the edge of Veterans Park. On the way back, you can cross the walk bridge at Ann Morrison Park and follow the pathway on the south side of the river for variety.

Directions: Head west on the greenbelt and drop under the 9th Street Bridge. You'll cruise along the greenbelt parkway across the river from Ann Morrison Park. You'll pass under the Americana Bridge, a red steel walk bridge, the I-184 bridge, Fairview and Main, and then you'll emerge next to Quinn's Pond and the Boise River. This is a nice quiet spot along the path. Take a dip in the summer – it's a great place to swim. Keep going west to the Mile 2.0 sign or to the bridge entering Veterans Park (just a few tenths farther) and turn around. Retrace your steps to the walk bridge junction at Ann Morrison Park, turn right, cross the bridge, and head east on the Greenbelt toward BSU. Turn left and cross the walk bridge to return to the start by the Capital Bridge.

The Hike: This route might be a better running route than a hike because of its out-and-back nature. But Quinn's Pond is a worthy destination, and the underpasses make it fun.

The Run: This is a great noon-time lunch run just minutes from the downtown workplace. It's too bad you can't loop the whole thing, but you still get to return through Ann Morrison Park. – SS

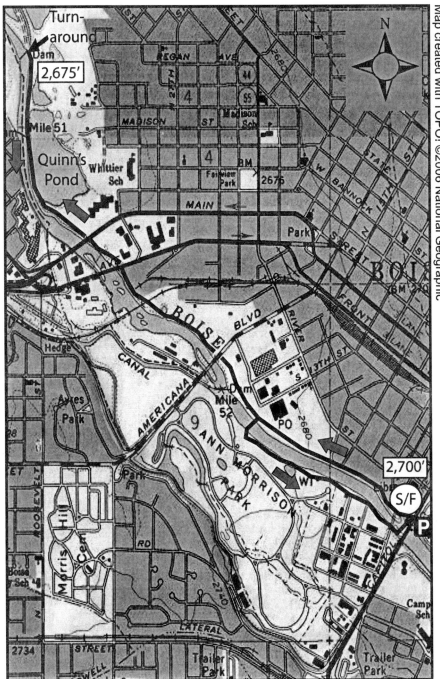

Map created with TOPO! ©2006 National Geographic

#6 Capital to ParkCenter Loop

Location: Boise River Greenbelt
Difficulty: Moderate
Distance: 4.5 miles
Tread: Paved greenbelt
Hiking time: 1:45
Running time: 45 minutes
Vertical gain: 30 feet
Watch out for: Wildlife, other greenbelt users
Water: Dependable in Boise River
Season: Year-round

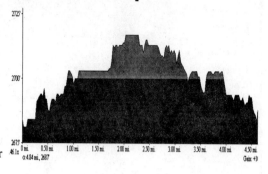

Getting there: In downtown Boise, take 9th Street south to River Street. Turn left on River and follow it over to Capital. Go across Capital on River and you enter Julia Davis Park. Turn right and find a place to park along the Greenbelt. Walk over to the junction of the greenbelt and the Capital Bridge. This is Mile 0. The hike/run starts here.

General notes: This is a perfect lunchtime running route for the weekend warrior, and it's a nice hiking loop for just about anyone. The route tours through Julia Davis and Municipal parks, a small piece of Warm Springs Golf Course, and then returns to town along the ParkCenter pathway and the river side of Boise State University. Great scenery the whole way, both natural and human.

Directions: Head east on the Greenbelt along the edge of the Boise River in Julia Davis Park. The trail winds through a normally shady area near the river, passes under the Broadway Bridge and then continues through a leafy area behind the Ram, office buildings and Fish and Game before you enter Municipal Park. Continue heading east out of the park. You'll skirt Boise Water Company's facilities and enter the east end of Warm Springs Golf Course. The path splits – take the right fork to reach the Park Center Bridge at mile 2.5. Now it's 2 miles back to Boise on the south side of the river, passing by office buildings in ParkCenter and then BSU. Go under the Capital Boulevard underpass, and then take the old steel pedestrian bridge back to the start. You can vary the route by crossing the BSU walk bridge on the way in or the way out.

The Hike: This is a fun greenbelt tour that features different views of the river and surrounding area. Watch for wildlife in the river and in the cottonwoods. In the summer, river floaters and tubers can provide great entertainment.

The Run: This is one of my favorite noon-time lunch runs just minutes from the downtown workplace. It's neat that you can experience greenbelt pathway on both sides of the river for the full length of the trip, while passing through two parks and BSU. Use the BSU walk bridge to vary the route, and try reversing the route, too. – SS

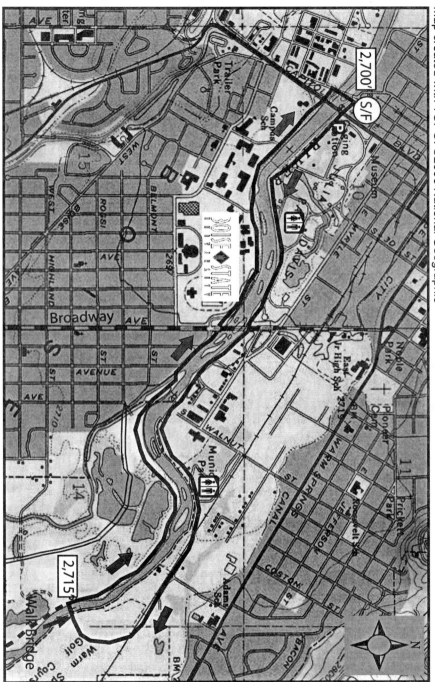

#7 Municipal Park to Barber Park Loop

Location: Boise River Greenbelt
Difficulty: Moderate to strenuous
Distance: 9.5 miles
Tread: Paved greenbelt and dirt walking path
Hiking time: 3.5+ hours
Running time: 1:35 hours
Vertical gain: 90 feet
Watch out for: Wildlife, bald eagles, other Greenbelt users
Water: Dependable in Boise River
Season: Year-round

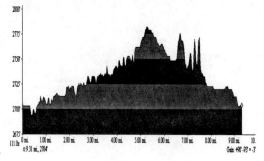

Getting there: From downtown Boise, take Warm Springs Avenue east to Walnut. Turn right on Walnut and go down the hill to Municipal Park. The hike/run starts here.

General notes: This is a scenic and stout Greenbelt loop. It's 9.5 miles to make the full loop, so that's a good day's hike or a pretty major run. It can be run in either direction, so if you tackle this one multiple times, reverse directions. If you're hiking, be sure to pack plenty of food and drink, and plan a lunch stop in Barber Park.

Directions: Start by picking up the greenbelt over by the river in the southeast side of the park, and head east. You wind out of the park, skirt Boise Water Co. and then run into Warm Springs Golf Course. East of the golf course, the path makes a straight-away bead for Eckert Road. Usually the wind is at your back, if it's blowing from the west, or it may be in your face. At the corner of Eckert, turn right and follow the path over to Barber Park. Turn right and head west on the dirt path closest to the river. It's heavily wooded in here. Watch for owls, kingfishers, herons and bald eagles, not to mention many songbirds. From the park, you'll continue west on a dirt walking path about three miles back to paved greenbelt behind the Cottonwood Apartments near ParkCenter. From here, you can follow the greenbelt across the ParkCenter walk bridge and return to Municipal Park that way, or take the long way around via the Broadway Bridge for the full 9.5 miles.

The Hike: This is a long but scenic greenbelt hike. It offers an excellent workout for power walkers and fitness buffs, too. Watch the tree tops for eagles and herons, and the river and its riparian area for other wildlife. To cut this hike in half, it's possible to shuttle a rig to Barber Park and enjoy the trip one way.

The Run: This is the highest-quality running loop in the greenbelt system because of the scenic area it tours and the fact that there is greenbelt pathway on both sides of the river for the full length of the trip. The long straight-away along Idaho 21 can be a bear in a headwind. Keep your eyes peeled for wildlife. – Boise Bs and SS

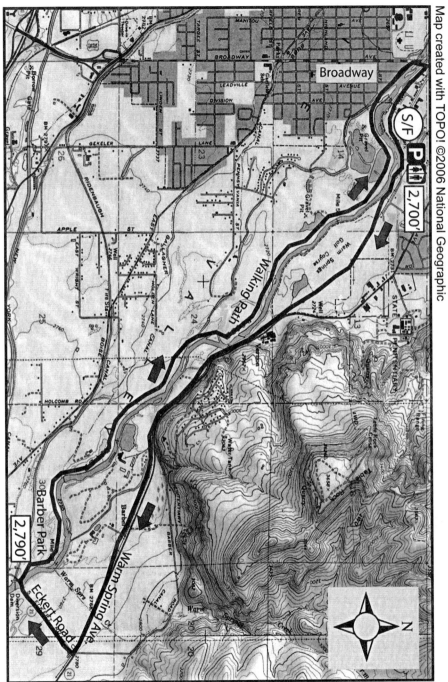

Map created with TOPO! ©2006 National Geographic

#8 Barber Park to River Run walking path

Location: Boise River Greenbelt
Difficulty: Easy
Distance: 3 miles
Tread: Dirt greenbelt path
Hiking time: 1:30
Running time: 30 minutes
Vertical gain: 39 feet
Watch out for: Wildlife, bald eagles
and tree roots
Water: Dependable in Boise River
Season: Year-round

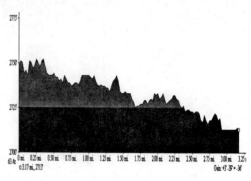

Getting there: In downtown Boise,
take Warm Springs Avenue several miles east of town to Harris Ranch. Turn right on
Eckert Road, and follow Eckert over the Boise River and take an immediate right into
Barber Park. The hike/run starts here.

General notes: The Boise River walking trail is one of the sweetest sections of the
Boise River Greenbelt. It's quiet, no bikes or other pavement-oriented users are
allowed, and the trail is located directly adjacent to the river, allowing for great
wildlife watching the whole way. Take your time and enjoy it. Bring some wine and
snacks if circumstances allow. There are benches in places where you can ponder life
and soak in the beauty. This hike can be shortened by leaving a vehicle at the east end
of ParkCenter Boulevard.

Directions: Head west on the dirt pathway close to the Boise River in Barber Park.
The trails braid as you work your way through the woods until you're far enough west
that the trail coalesces into one. Follow the dirt trail along the river for the next 3
miles. Ignore left-hand spur trails that connect to various neighborhoods. At mile 1,
you'll come to a corner where, in the winter, bald eagles often perch in a cottonwood
tree that overhangs the pool. Continuing west, you'll pass through a natural area next to
a mansion. The trail parallels Loggers Creek and a wide riparian zone. Watch for birds.
Eventually, the walking trail ends at the Cottonwood Apartments. Set up a shuttle or a
pickup.

The Hike: This is a beautiful hike at any time of year. Bring a fishing pole if you like.
It's also a great hike for kids in the backpack, and an awesome birding walk. Bring the
binoculars.

The Run: This is a great run along the Boise River. Watch your footing – tree roots or
rocks can turn an ankle. Do this run out and back, and you'll clock 6+ miles. – SS

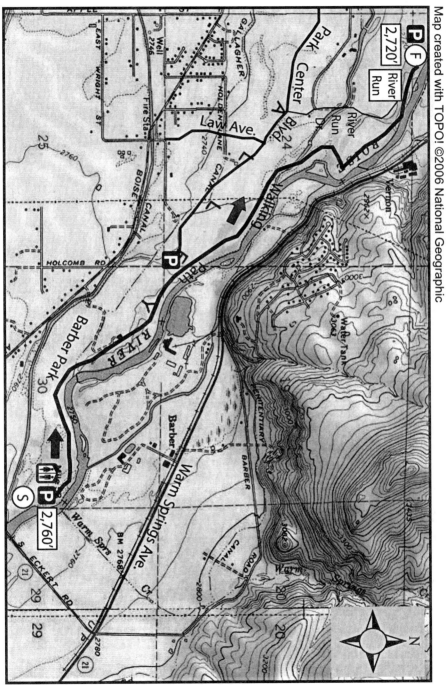

#9 Kathryn Albertson Park Loop

Location: Kathryn Albertson Park in Boise
Difficulty: Easy
Distance: 1.5 miles
Tread: Paved trail
Hiking time: 1 hour
Running time: 15 minutes
Vertical gain: 6 feet
Watch out for: Wildlife
Water: Dependable in ponds
Season: Year-round

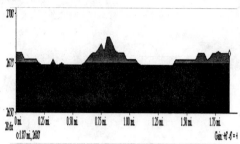

Getting there: From downtown Boise, take 16th Street south. The street turns into Americana Boulevard. Watch for a grand entrance to Kathryn Albertson's Park on the right-hand side, directly across from Ann Morrison Park at a stoplight. Turn right into the park. The hike/run starts here.

General notes: This is a beautiful place to talk a leisurely walk or run some loops for exercise. The 41-acre park attracts a great deal of wildlife, particularly waterfowl and songbirds. There are several spacious shelters to duck under if the weather goes bad or for shade. No dogs are allowed in the park March 1-June 30 during nesting season. At other times, dogs must be leashed. Joe and Kathryn Albertson donated the land for the park to the City of Boise; it opened in 1989. Watch for interpretive signs to learn more about habitat and wildlife. Be sure to bring the binoculars.

Directions: From the parking area, head into the park and follow the main pathway heading west along some trees, with a canal in the background. Ignore a left-hand turn in the first 100 yards and keep going straight to do the Figure 8 loop. It's about 8/10ths of a mile to the western end of the park. Take a primitive side trail over to the banks of the canal if you wish. Continue on the main trail as it bends back toward the east. Bear right to stay on the outer loop trail next to a large pond with an island. In a quarter-mile, you'll come to a T junction; bear right to stay on the outer loop. The trail passes by the Rookery Gazebo and an exhibit on the world's largest ponderosa pine from Idaho. Cool stuff. Keep going east on the outer loop and the trail wraps back toward the parking lot. Turn left to take an inner tour of the park and head toward the western end of the park again, staying in the center path between the ponds. Turn right at the western side of the park and loop back on the outer loop trail. You'll finish at 1.5 to 1.8 miles, depending on the loop configurations.

The Hike: Take your time, watch for wildlife and check out the shelters, especially the huge pine tree.

The Run: This is a quickie, even as a double loop. Cross over Americana to Ann Morrison Park and run a loop around the park to add mileage to your workout. – SS

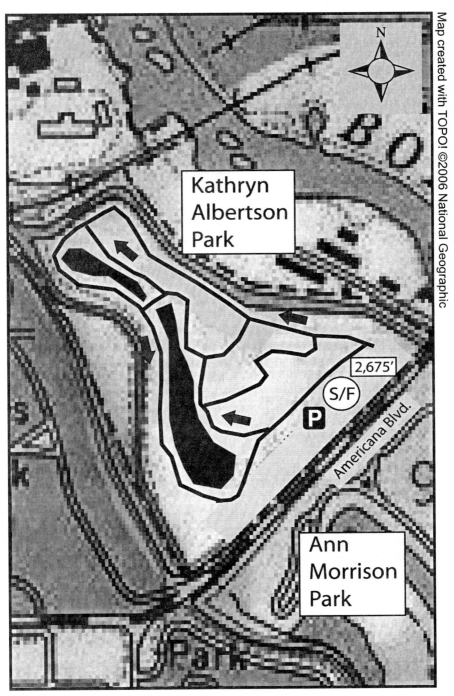

#10 Eckert Road to Lucky Peak

Location: Boise River Greenbelt, east of Boise
Difficulty: Moderate
Distance: 4.6 miles
Tread: Paved Greenbelt
Hiking time: 2 hours
Running time: 50 minutes
Vertical gain: 42 feet
Watch out for: Wildlife, bald eagles, other greenbelt users
Water: Dependable in Boise River
Season: Year-round

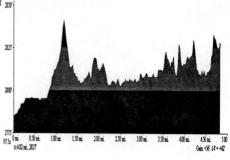

Getting there: From downtown Boise, take Warm Springs Avenue east of Boise about 4.5 miles to a right-side pullout/parking area next to old Eckert Road. The hike/run starts here. **Shuttle**: Leave a vehicle at Discovery Park, 5 miles ahead on Idaho 21.

General notes: This section of the Boise River Greenbelt is used most frequently by cyclists who are cruising out to Lucky Peak at fast speeds, roller bladers, and a few hikers and runners. So if you're running or walking with tunes, be alert for cyclists coming up from behind. It's a very gradual uphill tilt to Discovery Park, but the path bobs up and down in several places along the way. The main issue here is a possible headwind. Prevailing winds come from the west, but during the winter, spring and fall, easterly headwinds can be at play. Watch for bald eagles in the winter, and golden eagles along the basalt cliffs in the spring.

Directions: Hop on the greenbelt and head east. The first section of the path along Warm Springs and Idaho 21 is the least scenic. You'll pass by Lucky 13, Riverstone School and the Idaho Department of Parks and Recreation, and then at mile 1.2 drop down along a canal next to big cottonwoods, a much more scenic and protected area. The Barber Pool conservation area is off to your right. A side trail leading up to the Crow Inn emerges at mile 1.6. If hikers need a drink or some shade, here's your chance. Keep heading east. You'll pass by Diversion Dam, the diversion for the mighty New York Canal at mile 3. Now the path runs immediately adjacent to Idaho 21 and the little reservoir backed up behind the dam for a mile and a half to the park.

The Hike: This is a cool hike, especially after the path drops along a small canal next to mature cottonwood trees adjacent to Barber Pool. Be sure to bring sun screen and a hat in the summer; in the winter, the wind can be cutting and cold, so dress warm.

The Run: The route from Eckert to Discovery Park is a fun one. Exposure to wind and sun can add punch to the workout. Remember, it's slightly uphill, so conserve energy.
– SS

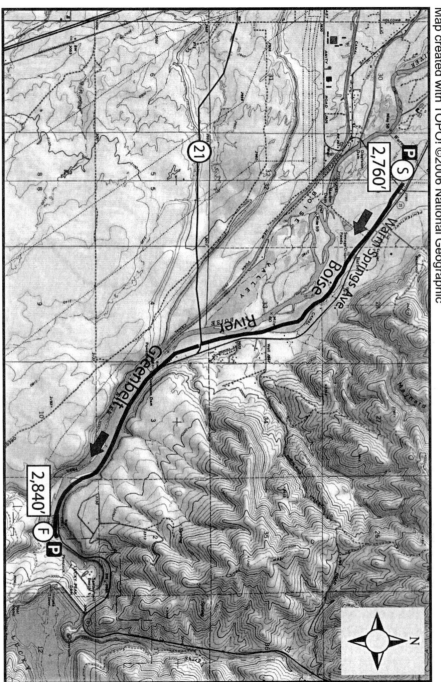

Map created with TOPO! ©2006 National Geographic

#11 Nampa Greenbelt

Location: Nampa Greenbelt in Nampa
Difficulty: Easy to moderate
Distance: 5 miles
Tread: Paved greenbelt
Hiking travel time: 2 hours
Running travel time: 55 minutes
Vertical gain: 36 feet
Keep an eye out for: Wildlife, other greenbelt users
Water: Dependable in Wilson Creek
Season: Year-round, depending on winter weather

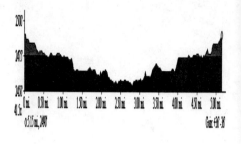

Getting there: From Boise, take I-84 west to Nampa. Take the Franklin Boulevard/City Center exit. Go left and follow Franklin to a junction with 11th Street. Turn right on 11th and follow it into downtown. Follow signs for Idaho 45 to Murphy to 12th Avenue South. Follow 12th past a big bend in the road to Iowa Street. Turn right on Iowa, and another right on Edgewater and pull over to park. The hike/run starts here.

General notes: It's worth the trip to check out the Nampa Greenbelt, also known as the Wilson Greenway. The pathway runs next to Wilson Creek, a creek/canal, through a

The Nampa Greenbelt.

number of nice neighborhoods with grass and landscaping along the way. This description provides an out and back trip on the most complete and continuous section of the pathway. There are other segments of the path off of 12th south of Mercy Medical Center near Greenhurst Road that extend over to Sunnyside Road. It'll be nice as the City of Nampa grows to see more miles added to their greenbelt system. Bring a leash and poop bags for your dog.

Directions: Hop on the greenbelt trail at the portal along Iowa Street next to the canal and go west on the trail. You'll pass a couple bridges in the next half mile or so. The trail winds along the creek for 1.7 miles until it intersects with Roosevelt Street. Cross Roosevelt and go left and pick up the path again and follow it to the temporary dead-end at Freemont Street at mile 2.5. Turn around and retrace your steps.

The Hike: This is a great place to walk with your sweetheart, the kids, whomever. You could run a shuttle to avoid going out and back.

The Run: It's a neat change of pace to run along the Nampa Greenbelt. Keep an eye out for bikes and other trail users. – SS

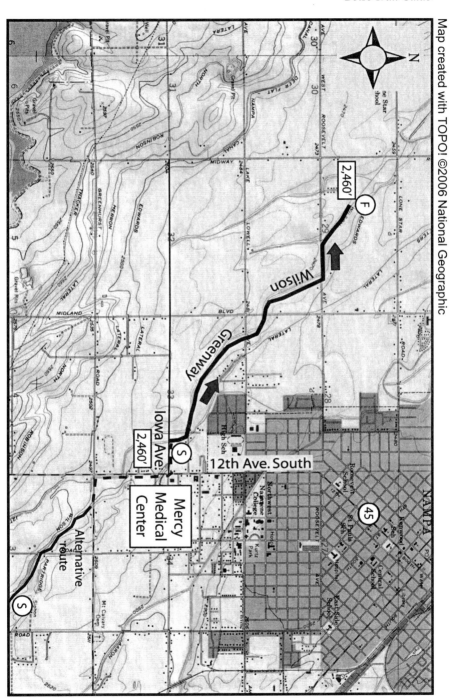

Boise Trail Guide

#12 Caldwell Greenbelt

Location: City of Caldwell
Difficulty: Easy
Distance: 3.7 miles
Tread: Paved greenbelt
Hiking time: 1:30 hours
Running time: 35 minutes
Vertical gain: 17 feet
Keep an eye out for: Wildlife, other Greenbelt users
Water: Dependable in Boise River and fishing ponds
Season: Year-round

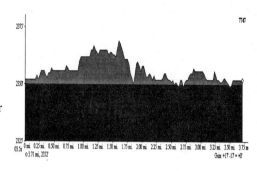

Getting there: Take I-84 to Caldwell and take the third exit as you're traveling west. Turn left on Centennial Way, cross the freeway, and watch for a park on the right. Turn right on Chicago, and then an immediate right into the park. The hike/run starts here.

General notes: The Caldwell Greenbelt is worth checking out. It's a 3.7-mile loop, including a trip around the Caldwell Rotary Pond. The route follows the Boise River upstream for a bit, ducks under I-84, and continues upriver to a bridge, where you cross the river and head back downstream along some fishing ponds. Take a victory lap around Caldwell Rotary Pond after doing the greenbelt loop to get the full mileage.

Directions: Pick up the greenbelt path behind a red gate at the northwest edge of the parking area and cruise up the trail. Keep your head down as you pass under I-84. The trail goes for another mile upstream to a point where it pops out on the road. Go left, cross the bridge, and turn left again on the path, going downstream now. The trail exits

The Caldwell Greenbelt.

on a road. Keep going straight along the ponds to a T junction. There's a sign for the trail, saying "Greenbelt Access Courtesy of Caldwell Camp Caldwell." Follow the trail around the ponds, duck under the freeway, and head back toward the park. The path runs along a road leading to Caldwell Rotary Pond. Turn right at the entrance to the pond (Mile 2.7), and follow the pathway 1 mile around the pond and return to the

parking area to finish at 3.7 miles.
The Hike: This is a nice quiet area along the Boise River, so it's very pleasant for a walk with your honey, your family or your dog.
The Run: This is a nice loop for a 3-miler. You can double it, and run it in reverse, if you're looking to increase mileage. – SS

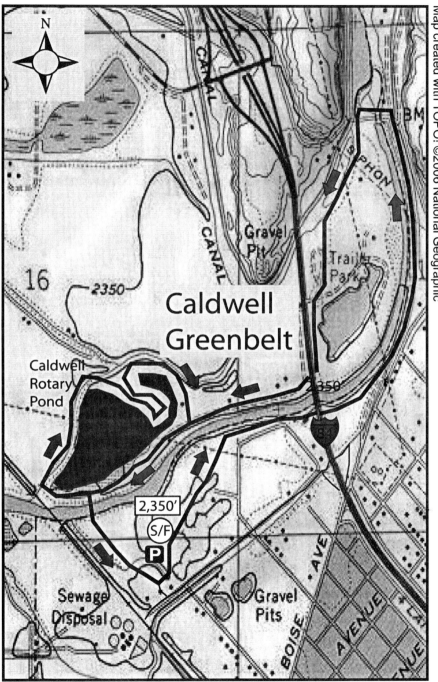

Easy Mountain Trails

13. Veterans - Big Springs Loops (p. 54)
14. Seaman's Gulch Double Loop (p. 56)
15. Camelsback Kids Special (p. 58)
16. Red Fox - Owls Roost Loop (p. 60)
17. Military Reserve Easy Double Loop (p. 62)
18. Castle Rock Loop (p. 64)
19. Surprise Valley - Oregon Trail Loop (p. 66)
20. Quickest way to Heaven at Bogus Basin (p. 68)
21. Beaver Creek - Crooked River Trail (p. 70)
22. Cougar Loop - Lehn's Loop (p. 72)
23. Blue Lake Family Special (p. 74)
24. Bruneau Sand Dunes (p. 76)
25. Jump Creek Canyon (p. 78)

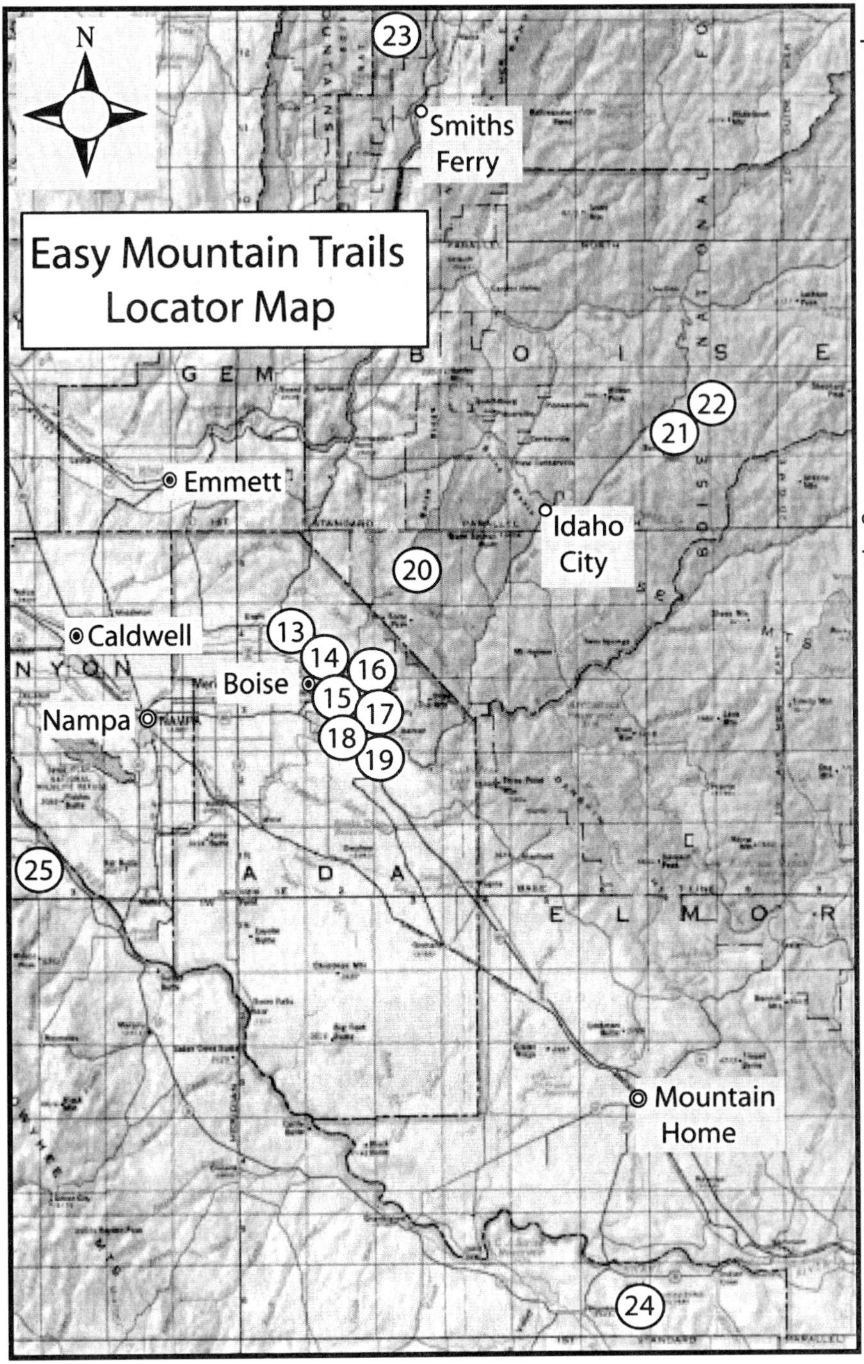

N

Easy Mountain Trails Locator Map

23

Smiths
Ferry

GEM

B O I S E

22
21

Emmett

Idaho
City

20

Caldwell

13

N Y O N

14

Boise

16

15

17

Nampa

18

19

A D A

25

E L M O R

Mountain
Home

24

Map created with TOPO! ©2006 National Geographic

#13 Veterans - Big Springs Loop

Location: West Boise Foothills
Difficulty: Moderate
Distance: 2.4 miles
Tread: Singletrack
Hiking time: 1 hour
Running time: 25 minutes
Vertical gain: 367 feet
Watch out for: Mountain bikers and other trail users
Water: None
Season: Late March - October; winter use may be doable, too.

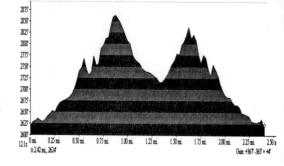

Getting there: From downtown Boise, take W. State Street several miles to Gary Lane. Turn right, take Gary Lane to Hill Road. Go straight and proceed toward Hidden Springs and the Ada County Landfill, until you come to old Hill Road before the canal. Turn left and follow Hill Road to the signed turnoff for Dry Creek Cemetery. Turn right and then immediately peel off to the right onto a dirt road leading to the Veterans Trailhead. The hike/run starts here.

General notes: The Veterans - Big Springs Loop is a nifty little double-pull neighborhood loop trail, and a fairly new addition to the Ridge to Rivers Trail System. It's a great loop for walking the dog, hiking with kids (in or out of backpack), or a quick 25-minute run. For a change of pace, it's worth checking out Veterans and Big Springs Trails. Other unofficial trails run adjacent to these trails, including a trail that climbs to the ridge next to the Ada County Landfill. This may or may not be recommended, depending on the direction of wind currents.

Directions: Follow Veterans Trail #114, a two-track road to start with, up the gulch. Within 100 yards, the trail dissolves into singletrack and winds up toward the ridgetop, where Veterans merges with Big Springs Trail #113 at mile .85. Go straight on Big Springs Trail. Ignore a left-hand turnoff for Veterans Trail, so you can take the long way around on Big Springs. You drop off the ridge down to the base of the housing area, and climb to the ridge again. Bear right at the ridgetop, and follow Veterans back to the trailhead.

The Hike: Enjoy a little fresh air while you walk your dog, take a casual walk or power walk the loop.

The Run: Strong runners will complete the loop faster than 25 minutes. You can lengthen the route by running along Hill Road or the canal path. – SS

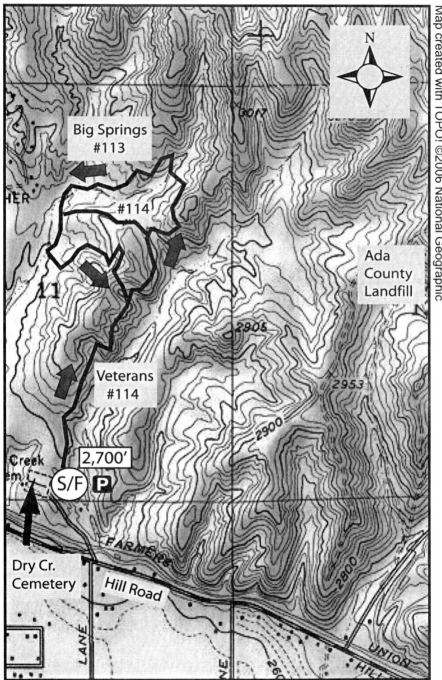

Big Springs
#113

#114

Ada
County
Landfill

11

Veterans
#114

2,700'

Creek

S/F P

Dry Cr.
Cemetery

Hill Road

FARMERS

LANE

UNION HILL

N

#14 Seaman's Gulch Double Loop

Location: West Boise Foothills
Difficulty: Easy to moderate
Distance: Loop #1, 1 mile;
Loop #2, 3 miles
Tread: Singletrack
Hiking time: 20 minutes to 1+
hours
Running time: Short loop, 10-
15 minutes; Long loop, 30-45
minutes
Vertical gain: 540 feet
Watch out for: Mountain
bikers and other trail users

Elevation profile chart: vertical axis labeled 3000', 2950', 2900', 2850', 2800', 2750', 2700', with 16.5x at bottom left. Horizontal axis: 0 mi., 0.50 mi., 1.00 mi., 1.50 mi., 2.00 mi., 2.50 mi., 3.00 mi., 3.50. Labels: 0:3.44 mi., 2782'. Gain: +539' -545' = -6'

Water: None. Dry route except for puddles in the spring
Season: Late March–November; winter use is feasible

Getting there: Follow Hill Road west of Boise past Gary Lane until you come to an intersection with Seaman's Gulch Road and Hill Road Parkway. Bear right on the main paved road and follow signs to Hidden Springs. At .9 miles from this junction, turn right into a parking area and trailhead. The hike/run starts here.

General notes: Call this one the quick-getaway double-loop special. The Seaman's Gulch trails are convenient to NW Boise and Hidden Springs areas. It's a great spot for a dog walk, a quick run or an invigorating hike at lunchtime or after work. On top of the ridge, enjoy nifty views of the Boise Valley. The trails are all singletrack – built by volunteers as part of a Ridge to Rivers-REI cooperative project.

Directions: Take off out of the trailhead on Seaman's Gulch Trail #110. **For Loop #1**, take the left-hand fork Trail #110 and climb to an initial ridge on a series of switchbacks. Bear left on top of the ridge on Phlox Trail #112, which comes up on your left. It's a short one-mile loop, which returns to the trailhead almost too quickly. Now ignore the left-hand turn after the start and follow Valley View Trail #111, **Loop #2**, around the nose of the ridge. It ties into Phlox at the ridgetop and you can head back to the trailhead. You've traveled 3 miles and scaled 540 vertical feet for a nice workout.

The Hike: Catch a little fresh air while you tour a finger ridge near the base of the Boise Foothills. Great place to take young kids, kids in the backpack or seniors.

The Run: The Seaman's Gulch Double Loop is ideally suited for a recreational runner because it's only 3 miles long and takes less than an hour. Still, you have to climb more than 500 feet, and that will cause a little pain. Stronger runners may complete the double loop closer to 30 minutes or less. – SS

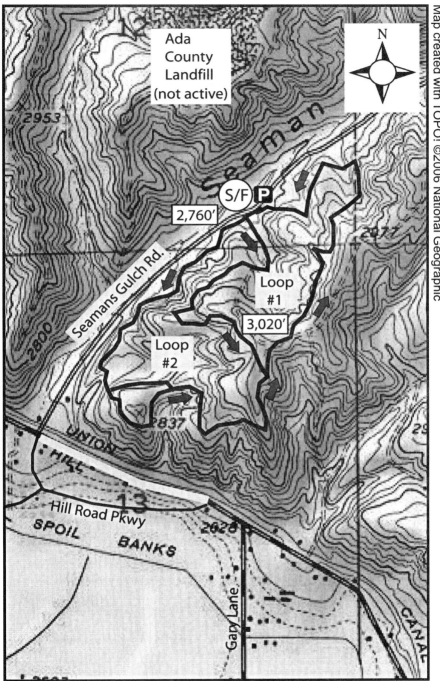

Ada
County
Landfill
(not active)

N

S/F P
2,760'

Seamans Gulch Rd.

Loop #1

3,020'

Loop #2

UNION

Hill Road Pkwy

SPOIL BANKS

Gary Lane

CANAL

Map created with TOPO! ©2006 National Geographic

#15 Camelsback Kids Special

Location: Boise Foothills
Difficulty: Easy
Distance: 1 mile or less
Tread: Singletrack
Hiking time: 1 hour
Running time: NA
Vertical gain: 1,149 feet
Watch out for: Other kids
Water: Dependable in Hulls Ponds
Season: Year-round

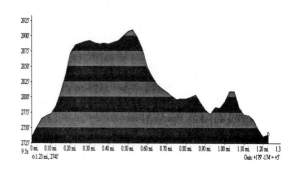

Getting there: From downtown Boise, take N. 13th Street past Hyde Park to Heron Street. Turn right and pull into the parking lot at Camelsback Park. The hike starts here.

General notes: The trails on the front face of Camelsback Park provide a great place for the kids to play in the dirt and sand. There are more gentle approaches to the ridgetop from the left and right side, and loops can be made between the ponds, Camelsback Ridge and trails on top of the ridge.

My boys climb the face of Camelsback.

Directions: Hike up to the top of Camelsback Ridge, either via the front face or the trails to the left or right side of the ridge. Your kids may want to scramble up the steep route, which is typical, and then they may want to run down. Let them play, while the rest of the family can hike to the top, cruise around the top of the ridge or fly a kite in the park. There's a great view of the city and the surrounding countryside on top. A nice loop can be made by taking Camelsback Trail #40 to the north and then drop down over to the Hulls Ponds to let the dogs get a drink of water. There's another sandy hillside that the kids love to play on over by the ponds. Return to the parking area when you've had enough fun.

The Hike: Bring a picnic lunch to hang out on the lawn at the park after your hike. If it's a windy spring day, a kite might be a good idea, too. – SS

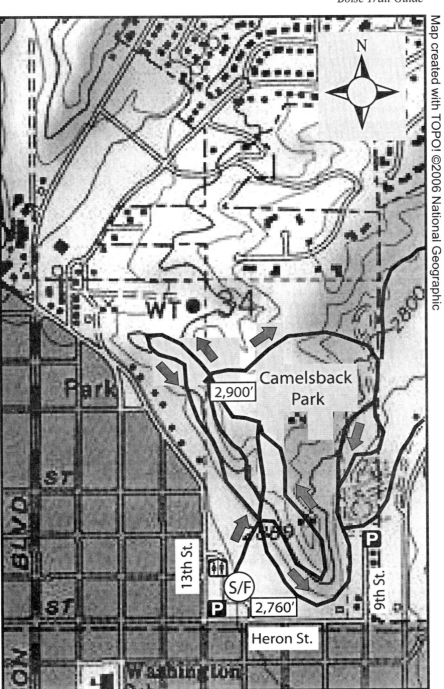

#16 Red Fox - Owls Roost Loop

Location: Boise Foothills
Difficulty: Easy
Distance: 2.3 miles
Tread: Singletrack
Hiking time: 50 minutes
Running time: 20-30 minutes
Vertical gain/loss: 197 feet
Watch out for: Mountain bikers
and dogs on the loose
Water: Plenty in Hulls Ponds;
seasonal in Hulls Gulch
Season: Year-round

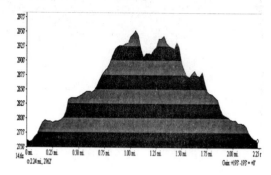

Getting there: From downtown Boise, take North 9th Street through Boise's North End
to a dead-end parking area on the eastern edge of Camel's Back Park. The hike/run
starts here.

General notes: This is an easy-going hike or run that still provides a nice relaxing
getaway close to Boise. It's a great one for packing infants in a front pack or backpack,
taking young kids on their first hike, or going for a short run.

Directions: Head north on Red Fox Trail #36. Climb a short, abrupt hill and then
follow the slightly uphill trail to a small summit. Drop down to and cross 8th Street,
pass through the parking area and pickup Kestrail Trail #39A. Follow Kestrel for less
than a quarter-mile, and turn right on Owls Roost Trail #37. Now it's an all-downhill
cruise on Owls Roost. Use caution when you cross 8th Street, and continue on the trail
back to the Hulls Ponds area and the trailhead.

The Hike: Enjoy this leisurely hike – listen for songbirds and watch for hikes. Look
for animal tracks in the sand and teach your kids how to identify critters. Be aware that
this is a very popular trail, and you will encounter lots of bikers, hikers, runners and
dogs on the trail. Say "Hi" to your neighbors and have a great time.

The Run: For those who are just getting into trail running, this is a perfect "beginner"
route. You can add difficulty to this loop by peeling off of Red Fox on Chickadee
Ridge Trail #36A to climb Chickadee Ridge and then drop back to Red Fox before you
cross 8th Street. Run this loop on a regular basis and you'll be ready to tackle longer
routes with more climbing. – SS

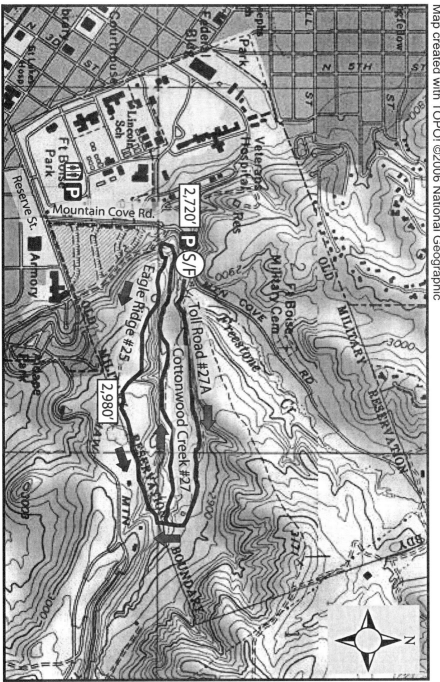

#18 Castle Rock Loops

Location: Castle Rock in East
Boise
Difficulty: Easy to moderate
Distance: 1.2 miles
Tread: Singletrack
Hiking time: 1:30
Running time: 55 minutes
Vertical gain: 300 feet
Watch out for: Other trail users
Water: None unless there's
potholes of water on the trail
Season: March - October; winter
use may be feasible when trails are
frozen.

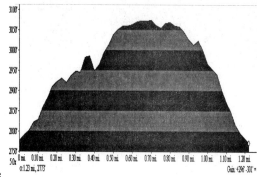

Getting there: From the intersection of Broadway and Warm Springs Avenue in east
Boise, go east on Warm Springs past the M&W market to Old Penitentiary Road. Turn
left and go straight toward the Old Pen. Turn left at the end of the boulevard and follow
signs for public parking by the Bishop's House.
The hike/run starts here.

General notes: The Castle Rock Loop trail is a
perfect hike for families with kids, and babies in
the backpack. If you have more time, you should
do the Table Rock loop, which is quite a bit more
strenuous. Once you've climbed to the top of
Castle Rock, kids love to play around on the rocks.

Directions: Head up Castle Rock Trail #19 and
climb one-half mile to the top of the spiky basalt
rock cap overlooking Quarry View Park. Turn right
at the top and take the Quarry Trail #18 along the
edge of the rocks (watch your footing), and
descend on Trail #15 back to the start. It's 1.2
miles to do the main Castle Rock loop. If you want
to do a second loop, take Castle Rock Loop Trail

A perfect hike for kids.

#19 at the base of Castle Rock and follow that around the edge of Quarry View Park
(on the flat) and then climb back to Table Rock. It's your choice on the way down.

The Hike: Take your time and enjoy it. Bring water and snacks for the kids.

The Run: This route is a quick but steep run for folks who like to run about 1 mile.
Master this route and work up to running Table Rock. – SS

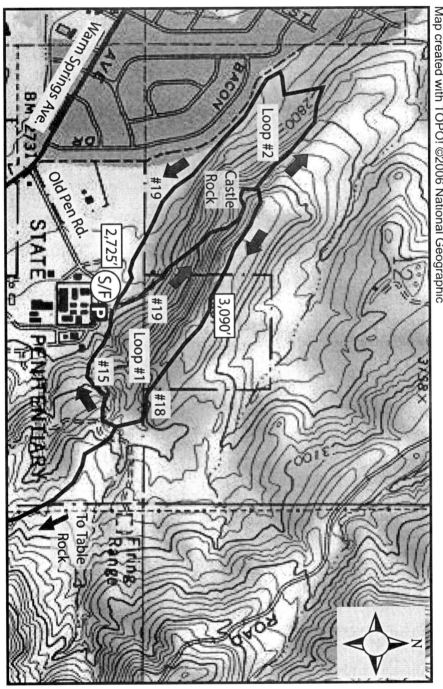

Boise Trail Guide

Map created with TOPO! ©2006 National Geographic

65

#19 Surprise Valley - Oregon Trail Loop

Location: Oregon Trail Reserve, SE Boise
Difficulty: Easy
Distance: 2.6 miles
Tread: Dirt road, singletrack
Hiking time: 1:15 hour
Running time: 25 minutes
Vertical gain/loss: 191 feet
Keep an eye out for: Other trail users
Water: None
Season: Year-round

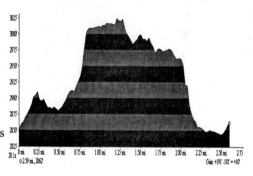

Getting there: From downtown Boise, go north on Broadway Avenue to the traffic light at Boise Avenue. Turn left and take Boise Avenue about 3 miles to a stop sign at Eckert Road. Turn right, go around the curve and then turn left on Surprise Way. Follow the road to Trinity Presbyterian Church on the right. The hike/run starts here. Public parking also is available by the Community Center and adjacent to Columbia Village on East Lake Forest Drive.

General notes: This is a neat loop that serves up a bit of history about the Oregon Trail while you get out for some fresh air and exercise. It's neat to walk/run along the base of the basalt bluff, climb the Kelton Ramp, where wagon trains used to descend into the Boise Valley, and then cruise along the edge of the rim with great views of the valley the whole way. Pay attention to dog regulations and please clean up after your pet. Bags are normally stocked at the Columbia Village trailhead.

Directions: Pick up the gravel trail at the base of the bluff and head east. It's about a mile to the Kelton Ramp grade. Thread around the rocks on the singletrack and then you'll pop out on top of the bluff. Turn right on top and follow Trail #102 that runs closest to the rim (for the best views) under the power lines. Pause for a moment to read the interpretive signs on Oregon Trail history. It's good stuff. The trail braids in several places as you head west. Stay close to the rim. At mile 2, you'll see a right-hand fork in a break in the cliff where you can descend back to the water tank. Take the dirt road going north from the tank out to Surprise Way and head back to the church parking area to complete the loop.

The Hike: This is a nice quick-getaway hike that provides nice views and some decent exercise, along with a dash of history.

The Run: This is a good running route that's very accessible to SE Boise residents. For others, the setting and history are worth checking out for a change of pace from other trails. – SS

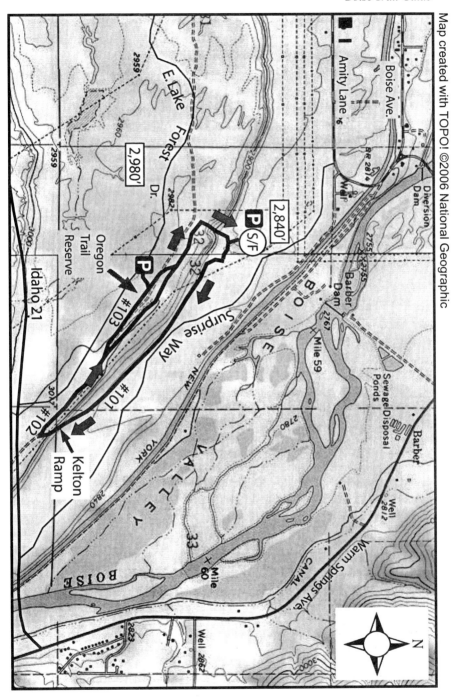

Map created with TOPO! ©2006 National Geographic

Amity Lane

Boise Ave.

Diversion Dam

E. Lake Forest Dr.

2,980'

2959

2959

2,840'

P S/F

P

32

32

Oregon Trail Reserve

#103

Surprise Way

Idaho 21

#101

#102

Kelton Ramp

Barber Dam

BOISE

2767

Mile 59

Sewage Disposal Ponds

Barber

NEW YORK CANAL

2780

VALLEY

Well 2812

BOISE

33

Mile 60

Warm Springs Ave.

Well 2862

3000

N

67

#20 Quickest Way to Heaven at Bogus

Location: Bogus Basin Mountain
Resort
Difficulty: Easy to strenuous
Distance: 3 miles
Tread: Two-track road, singletrack
Hiking time: 1:30 hours
Running time: 40 minutes
Vertical gain: 750 feet
Watch out for: Wildlife,
wildflowers, other trail users
Water: Fill up at Pioneer Lodge if
it's open; otherwise, it's a dry route
Season: June - October

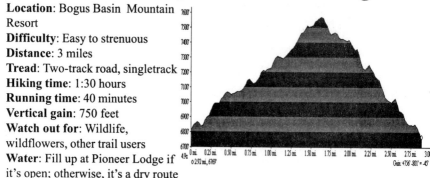

Getting there: From downtown Boise, take Harrison Boulevard north to Bogus Basin Road and Hill Road. Go straight (north) on Bogus Basin road for approximately 18 miles to the lower lodge. Pavement gives way to dirt for a short time, and then turn right on the signed paved road to the Pioneer Lodge. The hike/run starts at the lodge.

General notes: It's always a treat to climb to the top of a mountain and enjoy a 360 degree view. This route provides the quickest way to Shafer Butte summit, the high point at Bogus Basin Mountain Recreation Area. You start at 6,640 feet and climb a gradual contour two-track trail to the 7,582-foot summit. The trail gets steeper and more strenuous in the final approach. Take your time. Be sure to bring some food and favorite beverages for the summit. The downhill follows a steep sinewy singletrack back to Lodge Trail. Enjoy!

Directions: Head out of the Pioneer Lodge parking lot, climb to the top of Morning Star chairlift, and turn left on Lodge Trail #140. Follow the two-track trail on a slight uphill grade around the bend. Note the intersection with Tempest Trail #95, a singletrack on the right. This is your downhill route. Keep going on Lodge Trail to a junction at mile 1. Bear right and climb the switchbacks to the Shafer Butte saddle. Bear left here and climb to the top of Shafer Butte. Find a spot to sit and enjoy the view. Mores Mountain is the rounded peak immediately to the north, the Sawtooths are to the east, and Squaw Butte lies to the west. To return to the trailhead, go back to the trail junction at the saddle, and pick up Tempest Trail #95 next to the top of Superior Chairlift #3. Follow the trail down the mountain to Lodge Trail, turn left and return to the Pioneer Lodge parking area.

The Hike: This is a great hike for kids over 8 and just about any ability. But you've still got to climb about 750 vertical feet to the top. Take your time and enjoy it.

The Run: This one is short, stout and sweet. – SS

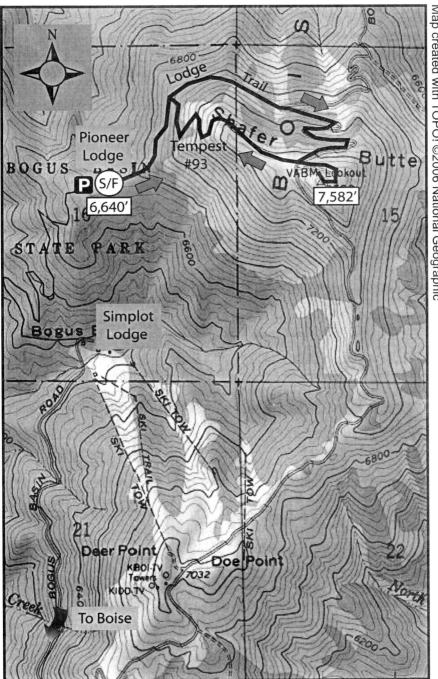

#21 Beaver Creek - Crooked River Loop

Location: Boise National Forest, NE of
Idaho City
Difficulty: Easy to moderate
Distance: 4-6 miles
Tread: All singletrack
Hiking time: 2-5 hours
Running time: 1:10
Vertical gain/loss: 175 feet
Watch out for: Horseback riders on
Crooked River Trail
Water: Yes, in Beaver Creek and
Crooked River
Season: June - October

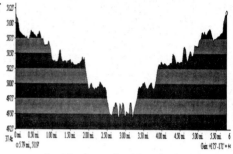

Getting there: From Boise, take Idaho 21 east to Idaho City. Continue east on Idaho
21 past Mores Creek Summit, Whoop-em-up Campground, and the Edna Creek Road
to a turnoff for the Beaver Creek Forest Service Cabin. Park in a pullout next to the
cabin driveway. The hike/run starts here.

General notes: The ideal way to do this one is to rent the Beaver Creek Cabin with
some friends and take a hike/run while you're there. The Beaver Creek Trail is a sweet
singletrack in a meadow that connects to the Crooked River Trail, another great
singletrack along the beautiful Crooked River. The Backcountry Horsemen and the
Idaho City Ranger District have been working on improving the Crooked River Trail
and adding bridges at stream crossings to make it easier for hikers/runners and
horseback riders. Bring a fishing pole if you like to fish. Bring food and water so you
can enjoy your day on the trail. Be sure to yield to horseback riders. Step off to the side
of the trail and let them pass. It'd be a good idea to bring mosquito repellant on this
hike. To rent the cabin, go to www.recreation.gov.

Directions: Head out of the parking lot and pick up the Beaver Creek Trail, a
singletrack, heading south across the meadow and then into a tight canyon. In a mile
the trail dumps out on the Edna Creek Road. Cross the road and the trail continues
along the Crooked River. You can go about 1-3 miles down this trail, turn around, and
come back for the easy route. More ambitious hikers/runners may want to go farther
downstream on the trail to add time/length to the trip. Just remember that it's going to
be uphill on the way back. The Crooked River Trail gets sketchier and less maintained
the farther you go. It's over 10 miles one way to the North Fork of the Boise River.

The Hike: Take your time and enjoy the hike.

The Run: This is a neat singletrack route, and sweet place to run in the forest. Watch
for and yield to horseback riders on the trail. – SS

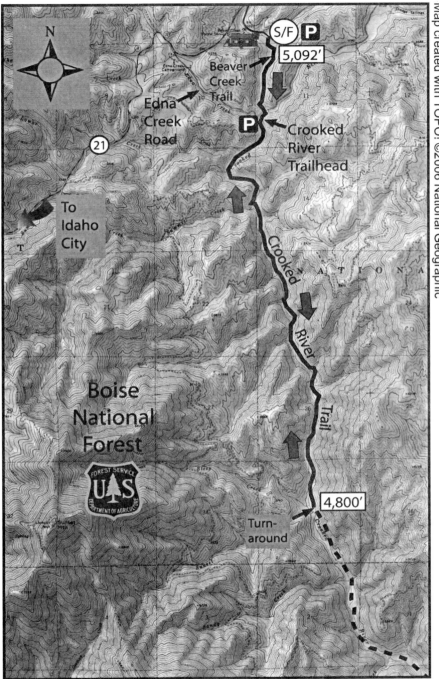

#22 Cougar Loop - Lehn's Loop

Location: Boise National Forest, NE of Idaho City, in Idaho City Park 'n Ski Trail system
Difficulty: Easy to moderate
Distance: Cougar loop, 4 miles; Lehn's Loop, 2 miles
Tread: Two-track, singletrack
Hiking time: 1.5 hours
Running time: 40 minutes
Vertical gain/loss: 246 feet
Watch out for: Other trail users
Water: Seasonal in small creeks and springs
Season: June -October

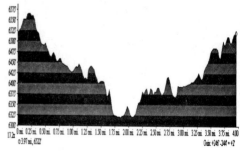

Getting there: From Boise, take Idaho 21 east to Idaho City. Continue east on Idaho 21 past Mores Creek Summit, Whoop-em-up Campground, and Gold Fork to a right-hand turn for Banner Ridge Park 'n Ski Area. Turn right on the 4WD road and climb a little over a mile to a point where the road levels out and park in a roadside pullout near the Banner Ridge yurt. The hike/run starts here.

General notes: The ideal way to do this route is to rent the Banner Ridge yurt and do some hiking or trail running while you're there. The Cougar Loop is about 4 miles long, and Lehn's Loop is about 2 miles. The main description is for the Cougar Loop, and then you can do a loop inside the loop by doing Lehn's Loop. Bring a Park 'n Ski map with you, because there are many other options available, including the Elkhorn-Alpine Loop (see page 114). These trails are best for hiking and running because they're singletrack. To reserve the Banner Ridge yurt, go to the Idaho Parks web site: www.parksandrecreation.idaho.gov or call 208-334-4199.

Directions: Head out on the dirt road going east for a half mile to a signed right-hand turn for the Cougar Trail. Go right and follow the Cougar Trail. You'll see a couple of signs for cutoff trails to Lehn's loop, if you want to do the loop within the loop. Otherwise, stay on Cougar for 1.5 miles. At the south end of the loop, you'll see a junction with the Beaver Creek Trail and another turn for the Elkhorn Trail. Turn right on Elkhorn to return to the Banner Ridge road. Turn right at Banner Ridge, and return to your vehicle. If you decided to include Lehn's Loop, you'll notch a total of six miles, depending on the configuration of your hike/run.

The Hike: This is an easy-going hike with only 246 feet of elevation gain on the Cougar Loop. Good hike for young kids and babies in the backpack.

Running notes: This is a nice shady running route in the woods at about 6,000 feet elevation – a great getaway when it gets hot in the valley. – Leo Hennessy and SS

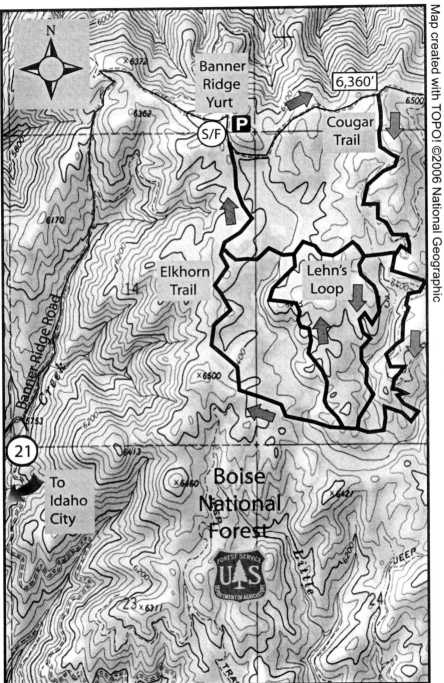

#23 Blue Lake Family Special

Location: West Mountain near
Cascade
Difficulty: Easy to moderate
Distance: 1.3 miles
Tread: Singletrack
Hiking time: 10-15 minutes one
way; 30 minutes round-trip
Running time: NA
Vertical loss/gain: 549 feet
Water: Dependable in Blue
Lake
Season: June - October

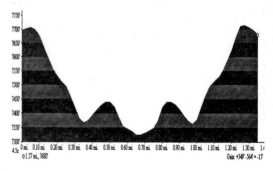

Getting there: Take Idaho 55 north, past Smith's Ferry, to Clear Creek junction
(Milepost 106.8). Turn left on Cabarton Road across from the Clear Creek bar/café.
Follow Cabarton Road past the Cabarton Bridge river put-in about 1.2 miles to

Dave Williams

Blue Lake is a great getaway.

Snowbank Road (USFS 435). Turn
left and drive up Snowbank Road
10.5 miles to a trailhead/parking
area on the right for Blue Lake. The
hike starts here.

General notes: The short hike to
Blue Lake is perfect for families
with small children or other people
who can't hike very far. The
Snowbank forest road takes care of
the elevation gain for you, so you
start hiking at 7,700 feet elevation.
It's an easy-going downhill hike to
the lake of .65 miles. Bring a
fishing pole if you wish. Be sure to bring food and beverages and enjoy your time in
the cool mountain air. After you're through hanging out at the lake, it's an uphill hike
featuring 549 feet of vertical gain back to your rig.

Directions: Head out of the parking lot and follow the singletrack trail downhill for .6
miles to Blue Lake. Head back the way you came.

The Hike: If you have time and the inclination, hike to the unnamed peak above it and
then cruise on the ridge spine over to Granite Mountain. You also could hike over to
the top of Snowbank Mountain or drop into several other lakes below Snowbank that
have good fishing. The Federal Aviation Administration operates a golf-ball shaped
tower on top of the peak. No public services are available. – SS

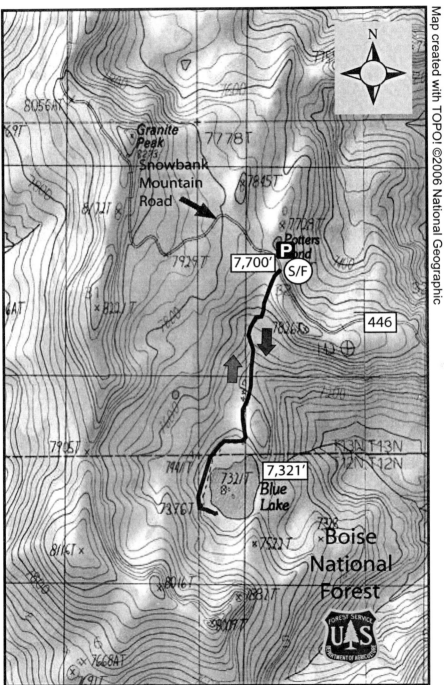

Map created with TOPO! ©2006 National Geographic

N

8056/T

69T

Granite
Peak
8293

Snowbank
Mountain
Road

7778T

7845T

7708T

Potters
Pond

7929T

7700'

P

S/F

446

8211T

7806T

79057T

7441T

13N T13N
12N T12N

732IT
8'

7321'
Blue
Lake

7376T

7338 Boise

7522T

National

8116T

8046T

8832T

Forest

FOREST SERVICE
U S
DEPARTMENT OF AGRICULTURE

8901FT

7668AT

79IT

75

#24 Bruneau Sand Dunes

Location: Bruneau Sand Dunes
State Park, south of Mountain
Home
Difficulty: Easy to strenuous, but
FUN!
Distance: 3-mile hiking loop; 5-
mile running loop
Tread: Deep sand and desert
hard pan
Hiking time: 1-2+ hours
Running time: 1:30

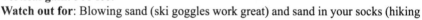

Vertical gain: 560 feet
Watch out for: Blowing sand (ski goggles work great) and sand in your socks (hiking
boots and bomb-proof ski gators work great)
Season: Year-round

Getting there: Take I-84 to the first Mountain Home exit. Turn right and follow Idaho
51 through the downtown core. A few miles south of Mountain Home, turn left on
Idaho 51 and drive south toward
Bruneau. Cross the Snake River, and
then take an immediate left on Idaho
78. Follow signs to Bruneau Sand
Dunes State Park.

General notes and directions: There
are many possibilities at Bruneau
Dunes State Park. It's a great place to
bring kids. Several small dunes are
immediately adjacent to the parking
area by Sand Dunes Lake. My map
suggests a 3-mile tour of the dune
summits, following the ridge spine
above the lake. But you may also
want to just play around in the dunes,

*Steve takes in the view on top of the dunes.
Note: He is wearing gators to keep the
sand out of his boots. It worked.*

ski or board the steeps or do cartwheels. It's up to you. Watch for interesting animal
tracks: Badger, coyote, muskrat, beaver, horse, porcupine, jackrabbit, raccoon, frog,
kangaroo rat, waterfowl, heron and magpie.

Five-mile run: Bruneau Dunes officials tout a 5-mile hike/run around the perimeter of
the park. Few people do it because it involves running across desert scrub country for
1.5 miles before you reach the dunes, and another 1.5 miles after you leave the dunes.
It's a slog. The route is depicted on the map. – SS

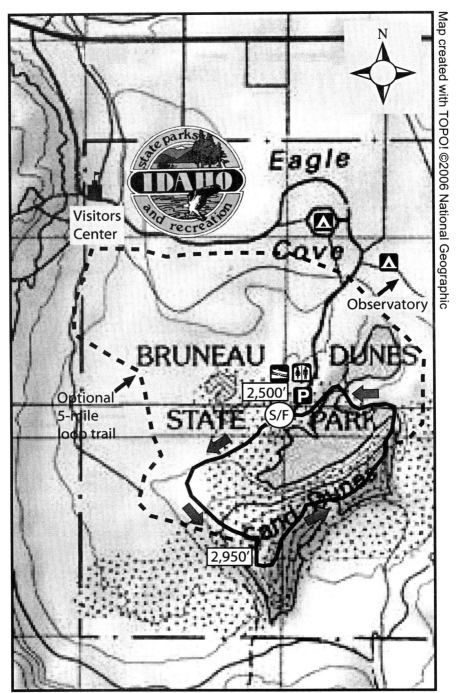

#25 Jump Creek Canyon

Location: 5 miles southwest of
Marsing
Difficulty: Easy to strenuous
Distance: .2 miles to Jump Creek
Falls; West Rim Loop, 1 mile
Tread: Singletrack and rock
scrambling
Hiking time: 5 minutes to falls;
hike time, 1 hour
Running time: NA
Vertical gain: 504 feet (West Rim
Loop)
Watch out for: Rattlesnakes and poison ivy
Water: Plenty below Jump Creek Falls
Season: April - October

Getting there: Take I-84 to the last exit in Nampa for Idaho 55 south. Follow Idaho 55 south to Marsing. Continue west, 1.5 miles past the junction with U.S. 95, to a T-junction with Cemetery Road. Turn left on Cemetery Road. In 1 mile, watch for a left-hand turn for Jump Creek Road. Head due south for Jump Creek Canyon, which is visible directly ahead in the Owyhee Foothills. Follow BLM signs as you approach the canyon to the lower parking area. The hike starts here.

General notes: It's an easy .2 mile walk to Jump Creek Falls. The most important aspect of the hike is to WATCH OUT FOR POISON IVY! It's everywhere along the trail, but avoidable by taking careful steps. Jump Creek glides about 75 feet down a basalt waterslide in a classic and beautiful canyon grotto. Bring a lunch and beverages and enjoy hanging out by the falls. It's a great place to bring kids because of rocks to climb on, small caves above the trail and swimming in the pool.

**Optional Hike: Falls Overlook - West Rim
Hike**: Start from the upper trailhead and follow the trail. There is an easy rock bouldering move to get around a small cliff in the first quarter mile. Follow the footsteps. When the trail bends right to head up to the West Rim, there is a left fork that leads to an adventurous steep downhill scramble to the brink of the falls, or hike to the West Rim. Pick your adventure. – SS

Funky rock formations are everywhere in Jump Creek Canyon.

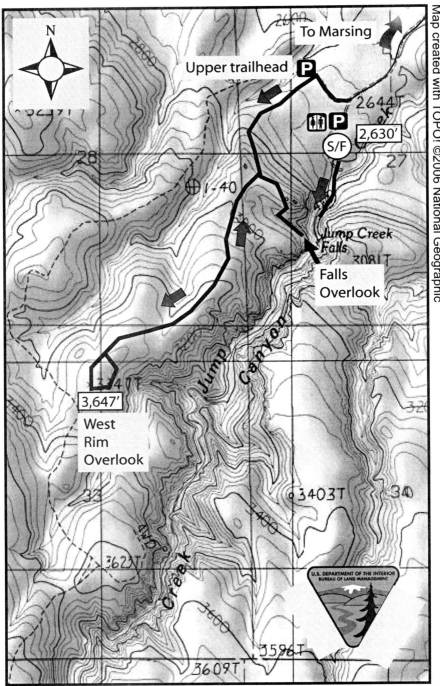

The Toll Road Trail in Military Reserve Park is part of Hike/Run #34, the Military Reserve Double Ridge Loop.

Moderate Mountain Trails

26. Eagle Foothills Little Gulch Loop (p. 82)
27. Hidden Springs Redtail Ridge Loop (p. 84)
28. Polecat Gulch Finger Ridge Loop (p. 86)
29. Corrals - Bob's Loop (p. 88)
30. Corrals - Hulls - Camelsback Loop (p. 90)
31. Dry Creek out and back (p. 92)
32. Kestrel - Red Cliffs Loop (p. 94)
33. Crestline - Hulls Loop (p. 96)
34. Military Reserve Double Ridge Loop (p. 98)
35. Military Reserve Two Coyote Loop (p. 100)
36. Shane's Loop (p. 102)
37. Orchard Gulch - Five Mile Creek Loop (p. 104)
38. Turner Gulch out and back (p. 106)
39. Bogus Basin Contour Special (p. 108)
40. Mores Mountain Loop (p. 110)
41. Idaho City - Charcoal Gulch Loop (p. 112)
42. Banner Ridge - Alpine -Elkhorn Loop (p. 114)
43. Station Creek Loops (p. 116)
44. Halverson Lake Loop (p. 118)
45. Wilcat Canyon Loop (p. 120)
46. Reynolds Creek Loop (p. 122)
47. Leslie Gulch Juniper Gulch Scramble (p. 124)

Moderate Mountain Trails
Locator Map

#26 Eagle Foothills Little Gulch Loop

Location: Eagle Foothills
Difficulty: Moderate to
strenuous
Distance: 5.25 miles
Tread: Two-track dirt road
Hiking time: 2:30
Running time: 1 hour
Vertical gain: 725 feet
Watch out for: Horseback
riders and other trail users
Water: Seasonal in Little
Gulch; otherwise none

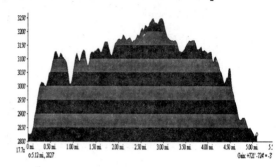

Season: March - November; winter use may be possible in low snow years

Getting there: From downtown Boise, take State Street west to Eagle. Turn right on Idaho 55 and go to Beacon Light Road. Turn left on Beacon Light and go to Eagle Road. Turn right and follow Eagle Road, which turns into Willow Creek Road, about 3 miles to a large dirt parking area on the right. The hike/run starts here.

General notes: Thanks to the generosity of two private landowners and the Idaho Department of Lands, I was able to include this route in the book. Please call the M3 Ranch Manger, as instructed at the trailhead, and ask for permission to use the trail. This route follows an old two-track road that tours the tops of the Eagle Foothills around the headwaters of Little Gulch. It's a cool hike and running route, especially in the spring and fall. It also may be possible to hike this route when it's frozen in the winter, depending on snow depth. **Caution**: It's possible that trail alignments and trail access in this area may change in the future. There are no trail signs in this area.

Directions: Head up the trail immediately to your left (north) from the trailhead and climb up a steep two-track to the top of the first ridge. Once on top, follow the two-track to the next ridge and go left. The two-track drops into a gully and climbs to the ridgetop again. This is the first of many dips where you lose elevation and climb a steep grade to regain the ridge. That's what makes this hike/run more strenuous than it may appear. Stay with the main two-track and ignore left-hand spurs that drop into the next draw to the north. After 2.5 miles, you'll see a major two-track peeling off to the left. Bear right and stay with the main two-track (more like six track). You're at the top of the Little Gulch now. The trail runs to the south for a mile before it bends to the west. Follow the two-track as it dips and climbs to the next ridge nose. Ignore small spurs to the left and right. By mile 4, you'll see the trailhead and the final descent.

The Hike: Bring a wildflower guide, a snack and water, and enjoy the scenery.

The Run: Pace yourself. There are lots of ups and downs between ridges. – SS

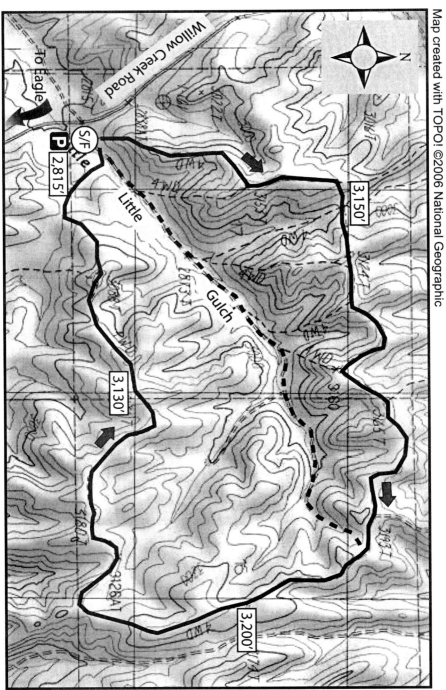

#27 Hidden Springs Redtail Ridge Loop

Location: West Boise Foothills
Difficulty: Moderate with
strenuous climbing
Distance: 3.4 miles
Hiking time: 1:15
Running time: 45 minutes
Vertical gain/loss: 575 feet
Watch out for: Mountain bikers
and dogs on the loose.
Water: Seasonal in Current
Creek
Season: March – October;
winter use may be feasible when trails are frozen

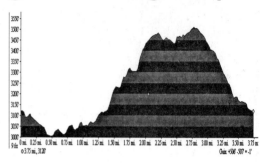

Getting there: Follow Hill Road west of Boise past Gary Lane until you come to an intersection with Seaman's Gulch Road and Hill Road Parkway. Bear right on the main paved road and follow signs to Hidden Springs. At the Hidden Springs junction, go straight and then right on Dry Creek Road to Cartwright Road. Go left and proceed .5 miles to the trailhead, a pullout on the left. The hike/run starts here.

General notes: The Redtail Trail is a scenic singletrack loop nestled in grassy foothills immediately north of Hidden Springs. It's a great trail for seeing wildflowers in the spring. The climb is worth it to reach the top of Smith Peak, where you can take in beautiful views of the mountains and the city.

Directions: Follow Current Creek Trail .48 miles to the Redtail Trail junction at the bridge. Go right, cross the bridge and follow Redtail up the hill. It's 1.9 miles uphill to the top. Watch for a thin vertical trail sign with an arrow that directs you downhill. It's worth the extra .1 mile to head over to the top of Redtail Ridge to soak in the views and catch a breath before continuing on Redtail downhill. Follow the trail .6 miles to Cartwright Road. Turn right on Cartwright Road and head back to the trailhead, 1 mile.

The Hike: This is a sweet hike with 575 feet of vertical gain to the top of Redtail Ridge. The trail climbs at a moderate pace that's doable for darn near anyone. Great hike for kids or babies in the backpack.

The Run: The Current Creek-Redtail Loop is ideally suited for a cross-country runner. The uphill and downhill are steep. I prefer to run this trail in the opposite direction as described above to reduce the steep uphill run. (You'll run just over 1 mile uphill, instead of almost 2 going the other direction). It's a perfect training run. If the loop seems too short, you can run reverse course, and do it again for a 7-mile workout.
– Tricia Keener Blaha and SS

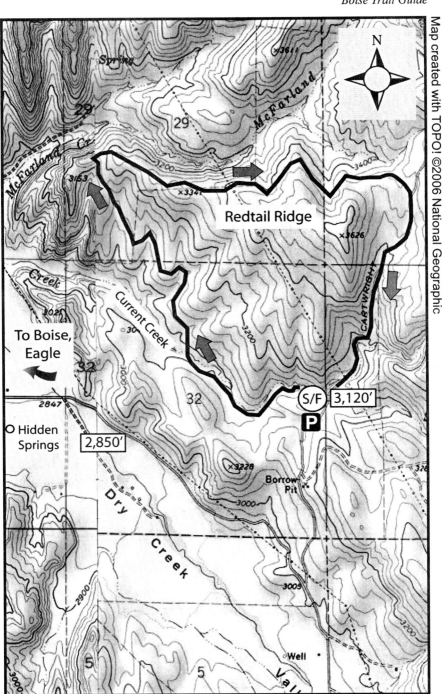

#28 Polecat Gulch Finger Ridge Loop

Location: NW Boise Foothills
Difficulty: Easy to moderate
Distance: 4.75 miles
Tread: Singletrack
Hiking time: 2 hours
Running time: 55 minutes
Vertical gain/loss: 812 feet
Watch out for: Mountain bikers
Water: None
Season: March - October; winter use
may be feasible when trails are frozen.

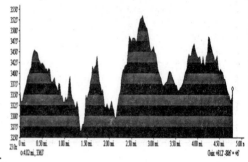

Getting there: Follow Hill Road west of Bogus Basin Road to Pierce Park. Turn right and go to the junction with Cartwright Road. Bear right on Cartwright and proceed to the Polecat Gulch Trailhead on the right. The hike/run starts here.

General notes: Trails in the Polecat Gulch area were a new addition to the Ridge to Rivers Trail System in Fall 2007. Funds from the $10 million Foothills levy were used to purchase the Polecat Gulch Reserve and establish a new trail system in it. The description here provides a full tour of Polecat Gulch.

Directions: Head up the Polecat Gulch Loop Trail, heading east (left). The trail climbs at a moderate pace for a quarter-mile to a ridge overlooking the Stewart Gulch Valley and the Terteling Ranch. Go left at the juntion with Doe Ridge, and stay with the Polecat Loop Trail. The trail descends to the toe of a ridge, before climbing again to the main ridge overlooking Polecat Gulch. Follow the loop trail into the gulch, and then climb Quick Draw back to the ridgetop. Bear left on Doe Ridge to keep your elevation and then go right on Polecat Loop trail. Now trail bobs up and down over four finger ridges before returning to the trailhead. If you take Polecat Loop instead of Quick Draw in the bottom of the gulch, it will add another mile to the trip. All of the trail junctions are well-signed and marked.

The Hike: This is an easy-going moderate hike on the ridge fingers that overlook Polecat Gulch. Even though the vertical gain chart makes it look as though the climbs and descents are steep, they are quite moderate. Hikers might even get a bit frustrated that the trail doesn't get to the high points faster than it does.

The Run: The Polecat Gulch loop provides a great tour of the gulch while providing an excellent workout over 4+ miles. The contour-nature of the trail makes the trail-running experience quite fun and easy going for the most part. – SS

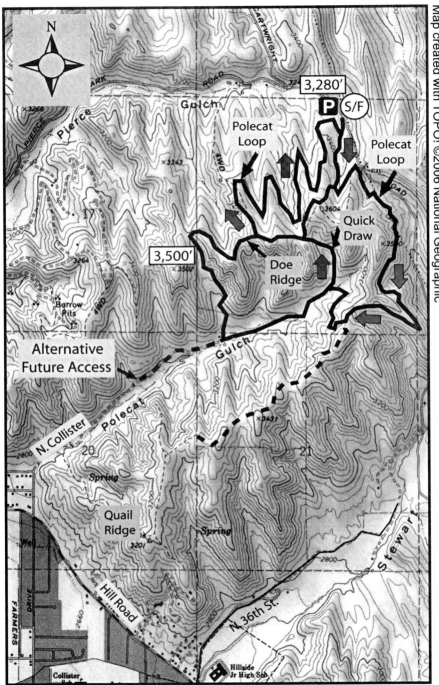

#29 Corrals - Bob's Loop

Location: Boise Central Foothills
Difficulty: Easy to strenuous
Distance: 6.25 miles
Tread: Two-track; singletrack
Hiking time: 2:30
Running time: 1:20
Vertical gain/loss: 983 feet/1,229 feet
Watch out for: Other trail users
Water: Seasonal in Crane Creek
Season: March – October; winter use may be feasible when trails are frozen.

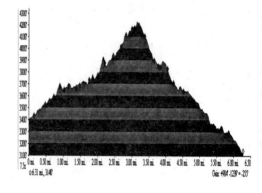

Getting there: From downtown Boise, take Harrison Boulevard north to Bogus Basin Road. Go straight on Bogus to the stop sign at Curling Drive and go 1.8 miles to the Corrals trailhead (parking pullout on left). The hike/run starts here. **Shuttle**: Plant a vehicle on Hearthstone Drive at the end of Bob's Trail. Take Bogus Basin Road north from Hill Road to a stop sign at Curling Drive. Turn right on Curling, and then turn left on Braemere. Go up the hill and turn left on Hearthstone. Follow it to the dead end.

General notes: Corrals - Bob's is a popular scenic route, with great views. Listen for songbirds along the creek and watch for hawks. The climb to Corrals Summit is pretty moderate until the last steep switchback. It's a fun rock-dodge cruise down Bob's. The trail is named for Bob Wood of Boise.

Directions: Head east on Corrals Trail #31. The trail wanders on a sandy two-track for the first mile or so. Pass through a gate and close it. Cattle graze in this area. The trail goes around several bends and dissolves into singletrack next to the creek. You'll pass through another gate, cross the creek and begin a steeper climb along the creek. An abrupt right-hand bend in the trail signals the final ascent to Corrals Summit. Once on top, ignore a left-hand junction with Scott's Trail, and climb one last short hill to the summit. Relax and enjoy the view. You've climbed 983 feet over 3.5 miles. Head down Corrals about 1 mile to Bob's junction. Turn right on Bob's and enjoy the downhill cruise on the rocky trail.

The Hike: This is a pretty easy-going moderate hike, but it's still 6.5 miles. Great place to bring dogs, or kids over 10.

The Run: Corrals is an enjoyable run because of its moderate grade, and the rocks on Bob's Trail keep you entertained. Watch your footing. Bob's is rated an advanced mountain bike trail because of many rock features, so use caution.
– Boise Bs and SS

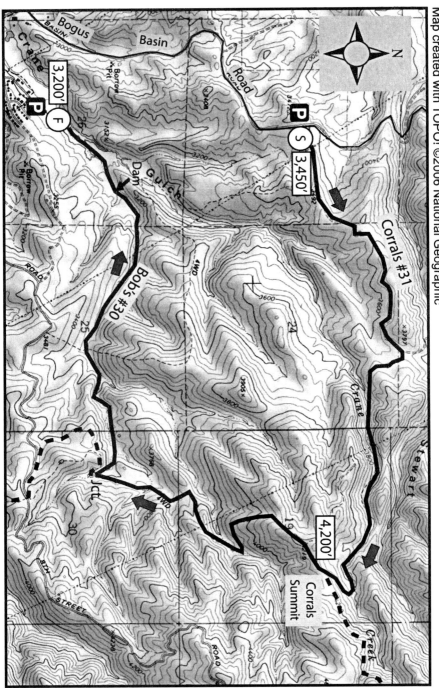

#30 Corrals - Hulls - Camelsback Loop

Location: Boise Central Foothills
Difficulty: Moderate, with strenu-
ous pitches
Distance: 9.25 miles
Tread: Two-track, singletrack
Hiking time: 4 hours
Running time: 2 hours
Vertical gain/loss: 1,100/1,716 feet
Watch out for: Mountain bikers
and other trail users.
Water: Seasonal in Crane Creek

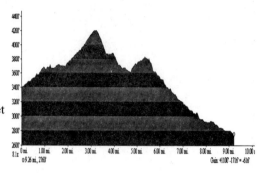

and Hulls Gulch
Season: March-October; winter use may be feasible when trails are frozen.

Getting there: From downtown Boise, take Harrison Boulevard to Bogus Basin Road.
Go straight on Bogus to a stop sign at Curling Drive. Go straight – it's 1.8 miles to the
Corrals trailhead (parking pullout on left). The hike/run starts here. An alternative
trailhead is ¼-mile farther up the road on the right. See map. **Shuttle**: Plant a vehicle at
Camelsback Park at the junction of 13th and Heron in Boise's North End.

General notes: This is a pretty major hike/run, but it's well worth the effort. It's a
scenic climb up Corrals, and then a fun cruise over to the 8th Street Parking Lot, before
dropping down Hulls to Camelsback Park. At 9.25 miles, this is a major day hike, and
a substantial run with 1,100 vertical feet of climbing and 1,716 feet of descent.

Directions: Head up Corrals Trail #31. It's about 3 miles to the Corrals Summit.
Ignore junctions with Hard Guy and Scott's Trail, and stay on Corrals. Take a moment
at the Corrals Summit to soak up the view. You'll descend a steep trail and then it's up
and down back to the motorcycle parking lot. Pick up Hulls Gulch Trail on the south
side of the parking lot and descend to the Crestline - Hulls junction, bear right on Hulls
and enjoy a downhill cruise on the rocky trail. At the junction with Redcliffs and Hulls,
bear right and follow Hulls to the lower parking lot. Cross 8th Street here and follow
Red Fox to Camelsback Park.

The Hike: Be sure to pack plenty of water and food for this hike. It's either an easy-
going 4-plus-hour hike, or a 3-plus-hour power hike. There's a good chance of water in
Crane Creek for dogs going up Corrals, and a good chance of water in Hulls.

The Run: Corrals to Camelsback is a long haul – 9.25 miles over 2 hours, depending
on your speed. Conserve energy and be sure to pack water. It's a rewarding workout,
though, because you'll burn a bunch of calories, and you'll tour a big chunk of the
central foothills. – Boise Bs and SS

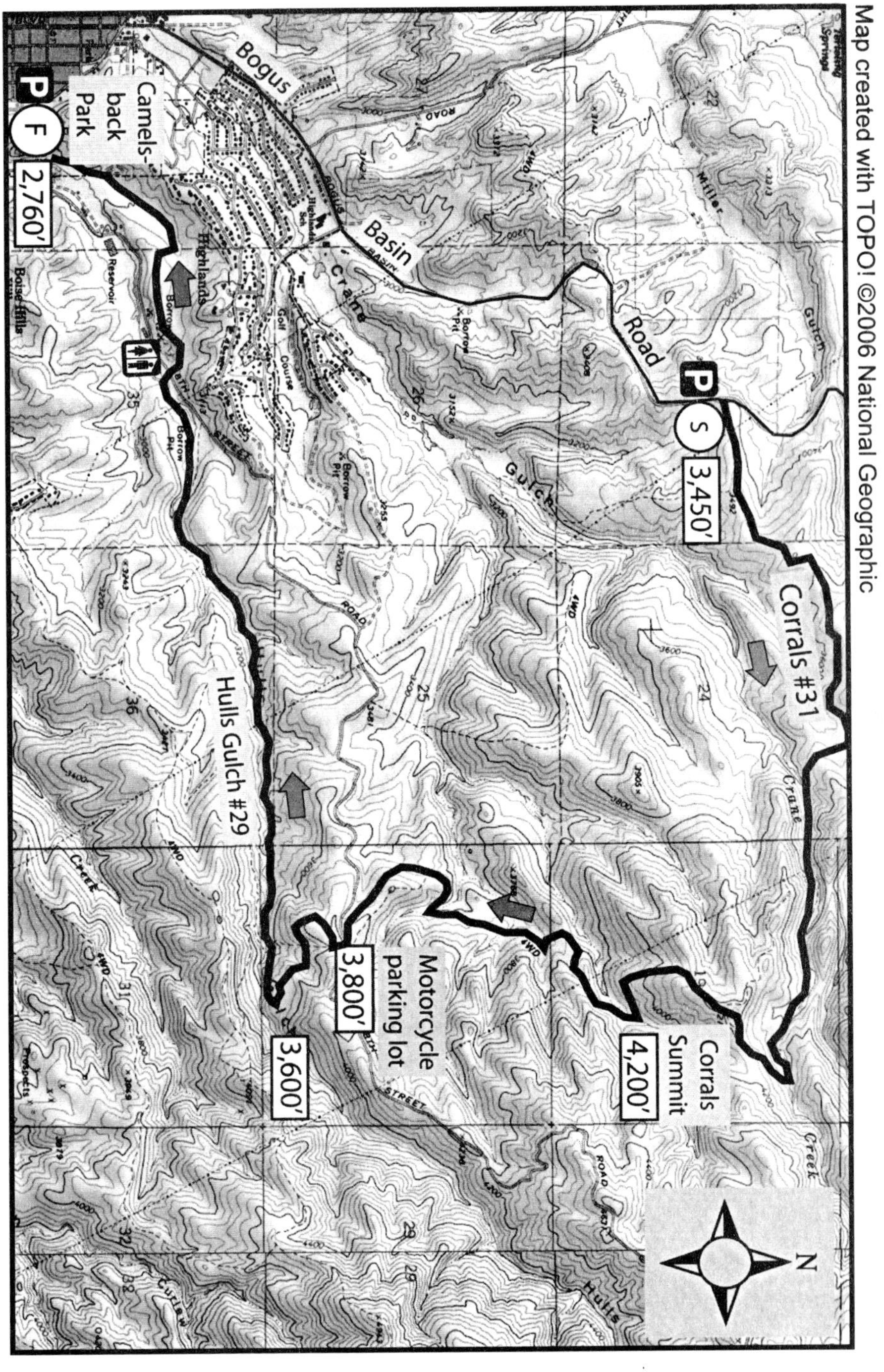

Map created with TOPO! ©2006 National Geographic

Camels back Park

P F 2,760'

Bogus Basin

Crane

Road

P S 3,450'

Corrals #31

Hulls Gulch #29

Motorcycle parking lot

3,800'

3,600'

Corrals Summit 4,200'

N

Boise Trail Guide

#31 Dry Creek out and back

Location: Boise Central Foothills
Difficulty: Moderate to strenuous
Distance: 6.85 miles to the top
Tread: Singletrack
Hiking time: 3 hours
Running time: 1:45
Vertical gain: 2,570 feet
Watch out for: Creek crossings
Water: Dependable in Dry Creek
Season: May - October; snow hike
in winter may be doable in the
lower end

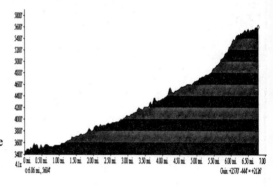

Getting there: From downtown Boise, take Harrison Boulevard north to Bogus Basin Road. Go straight and take Bogus, past the Corrals Trailhead, about 3 miles from the stop sign at Curling Drive to an unsigned right-side pullout on Bogus Basin Road. The hike/run starts here.

General notes: Dry Creek is one of the best creekside hikes in the Boise Foothills. It doesn't get that much use, and you hike into some beautiful secluded hideaways along Dry Creek, a stream that flows year-round. As you hike upstream, you'll experience a transition from a wide-open shrub-steppe sagebrush habitat to a shady pine forest. Be sure to pack food and drink and enjoy yourself. I've seen wild turkeys, ruffed grouse, blue grouse, deer and other critters along the way.

Directions: Follow the singletrack up the creek. The trail winds through egg-shaped granite rocks initially and joins the creek in less than a mile. Follow the trail upstream along Dry Creek as far as you wish. It's 6.8 miles to the Boise Ridge Road. There are only a couple of junctions along the way. The first one comes in a mile, where a cutoff trail on the right connects to the Hard Guy Trail. Keep going upstream along the creekside trail. The next one is at the junction with Shingle Creek Trail. Ignore that right-hand fork and keep going up the main trail. You may or may not wish to climb far enough to connect to a spur road that connects to Bogus Basin Road (at mile 5), or take Dry Creek Trail all the way to the Boise Ridge Road. Ambitious runners or hikers can turn right on the Boise Ridge Road and head over to Hard Guy Trail #33 and do a loop back to Dry Creek (14.2 miles total). That'd be a heck of a day trip.

The Hike: Reserve this one for a day when you've got some time to really enjoy the creekside trail and the surrounding countryside. Bring a lunch and plenty of water.

The Run: Most runners will scale the trail maybe 2-3 miles and run back. The full distance to the Boise Ridge is a challenging run, with gonzo steep climbs in the last two miles to gain the ridge. – SS

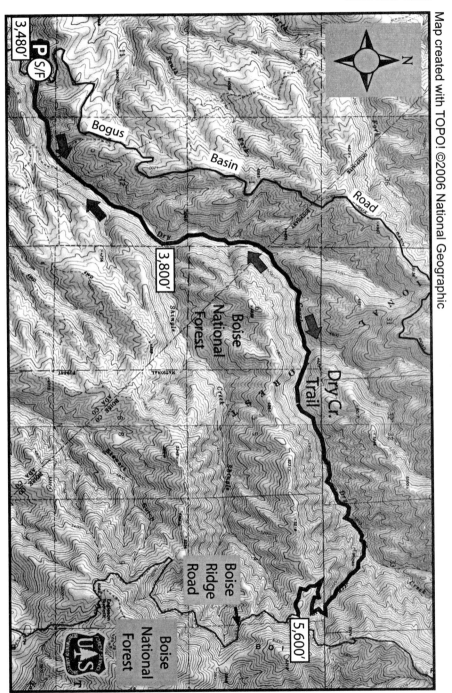

#32 Kestrel - Red Cliffs Loop

Location: Boise Central Foothills
Difficulty: Moderate to strenuous
uphill; steep downhill
Distance: 5 miles
Tread: All singletrack
Hiking time: 2-2.5 hours
Running time: 55 minutes
Vertical gain/loss: 606 feet
Watch out for: Mountain bikers,
dogs and other trail users
Water: Yes, year-round water in
Hulls Ponds by the trailhead;
seasonal in Hulls Gulch

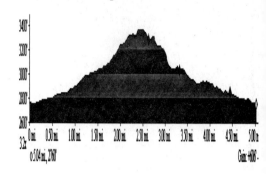

Season: March - November; winter use may be feasible depending on snow.

Getting there: From downtown Boise, take N. 13th Street to Heron Street, turn right and pull into the parking lot for Camelsback Park. The hike/run starts here.

General notes: This is a popular route in the Boise Foothills for hikers and runners. It's a cool loop trail with nice views of the valley. It's a perfect length for a lunchtime run, and it's a quality two-hour hike close to town.

Directions: Head east to the trailhead at the dead-end of North 9th Street. Veer right at Hulls Ponds and hook up with Owls Roost Trail #37. In 100 yards, the trail crosses 8th Street; continue on Owls Roost. At the next junction, veer left to hike/run through the cottonwood grove. At mile 1, the trail intersects with Kestrel, turn right and climb Kestrel to Crestline. It's about .6 miles of continuous climbing. Turn left on Crestline and proceed a few hundred yards to the junction on the left with Red Cliffs Trail #38. Turn left, and descend on Red Cliffs to Hulls Gulch. It's a steep, rutted trail in places. Watch your footing. Turn left at the junction with Hulls Gulch (mile 4), cruise to the 8th Street parking area, cross 8th Street and take Red Fox Trail #36 back to Camelsback Park.

The Hike: This is a great trail for a casual foothills walk with your friends, family, dogs, whatever. It's a steady climb up Kestrel, but you can moderate your speed.

The Run: From a running perspective, this is a popular standby. The moderate, slightly uphill cruise on Owls Roost is a nice warm up for the steeper climb up Kestrel. You can crank up the hill as fast as your lungs and legs will allow. After one more steep climb 100 yards after joining Crestline Trail, the trail is level for a bit and then it dives downhill to Red Cliffs. During periods in between spring melt and winter freeze, the footing can be tricky in steep spots. It's fun to wind around the lower toe of the ridge and then let it rip back to Camelsback on Red Fox. – SS

HARRISON BLVD

Hyde Park

S/F
P

2,740'

Camelsback Park

Borrow Pits

WT

Red Fox #36

Reservoir

Boise Hills Village

Owl's Roost #37

Jct.

Highlands

Borrow Pits

Borrow Pit

8TH

Kestrel #39A

Red Cliffs #39

Hulls Gulch

Golf Course

8th Street

STREET

3,290'

N

95

#33 Crestline - Hulls Loop

Location: Boise Central Foothills
Difficulty: Moderate, with
strenuous pitches
Distance: 7.25 miles
Tread: Two-track; singletrack
Hiking time: 2:30
Running time: 1:30
Vertical gain/loss: 868 feet
Watch out for: Mountain bikers
and other trail users.
Water: Dependable in Hulls
Ponds; seasonal in Hulls Gulch.

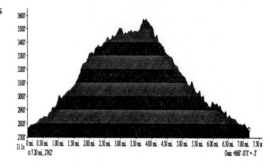

Season: March - October; winter use may be feasible when trails are frozen.

Getting there: From downtown Boise, take North 9th Street to a dead end parking area on the east edge of Camelsback Park. The hike/run starts here.

General notes: This is a classic loop in the Central Foothills. It may be one of the most popular loops, if not THE most popular loop, because it's a great tour in a scenic setting. The climb up Kestrel and Crestline is more gradual than doing this loop in reverse (climbing Hulls), so if you want to increase your workout, try it that way.
Directions: Head up Red Fox Trail #36. Turn right at the first pond, and pick up Owls Roost Trail #37. Climb the gradual uphill trail, cross 8th Street and pickup Kestrel Trail

Boise Bs scale Hulls Gulch.

#39A near the Hulls Gulch Interpretive Center. Climb Kestrel a half mile to Crestline Trail #28, commonly known as the Freeway. Turn left. It's mostly gradual climbing on the Freeway for about 2 miles to the Hulls Gulch junction. Take a breather. You've climbed nearly 900 feet over four miles. Turn left on Hulls and enjoy an all-downhill back to the bottom of Hulls. Cross 8th street by the parking area and take Red Fox Trail #36 back to the trailhead.

The Hike: This is a cool, but significant hike. Most people will take about 3 hours to do it. Power hikers will take about 2.5 hours. Because of the length of this route, it may be too long to take young kids in the backpack. Be sure to bring a lunch and water.

The Run: Weekend warriors love this run. It's a great workout because of the distance, and you get to enjoy the scenery along the way. After the grind up Kestrel, it's pretty easy going on the Freeway. Watch your footing on the way down Hulls because of rocks, sand and a few boulders. SS

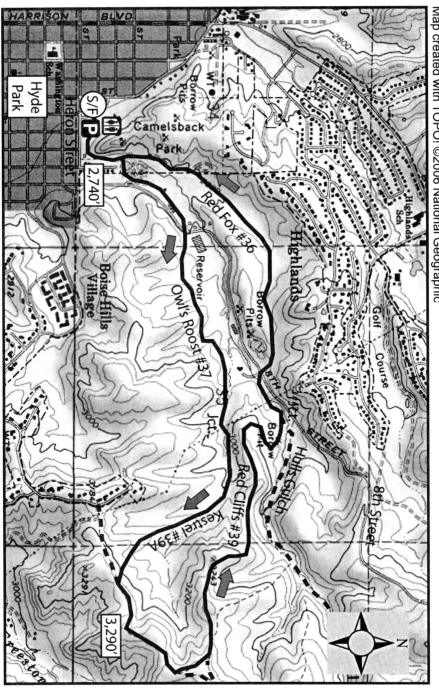

#33 Crestline - Hulls Loop

Location: Boise Central Foothills
Difficulty: Moderate, with
strenuous pitches
Distance: 7.25 miles
Tread: Two-track; singletrack
Hiking time: 2:30
Running time: 1:30
Vertical gain/loss: 868 feet
Watch out for: Mountain bikers
and other trail users.
Water: Dependable in Hulls
Ponds; seasonal in Hulls Gulch.

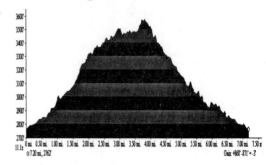

Season: March - October; winter use may be feasible when trails are frozen.

Getting there: From downtown Boise, take North 9th Street to a dead end parking area on the east edge of Camelsback Park. The hike/run starts here.

General notes: This is a classic loop in the Central Foothills. It may be one of the most popular loops, if not THE most popular loop, because it's a great tour in a scenic setting. The climb up Kestrel and Crestline is more gradual than doing this loop in reverse (climbing Hulls), so if you want to increase your workout, try it that way.

Directions: Head up Red Fox Trail #36. Turn right at the first pond, and pick up Owls Roost Trail #37. Climb the gradual uphill trail, cross 8th Street and pickup Kestrel Trail

Boise Bs scale Hulls Gulch.

#39A near the Hulls Gulch Interpretive Center. Climb Kestrel a half mile to Crestline Trail #28, commonly known as the Freeway. Turn left. It's mostly gradual climbing on the Freeway for about 2 miles to the Hulls Gulch junction. Take a breather. You've climbed nearly 900 feet over four miles. Turn left on Hulls and enjoy an all-downhill back to the bottom of Hulls. Cross 8th street by the parking area and take Red Fox Trail #36 back to the trailhead.

The Hike: This is a cool, but significant hike. Most people will take about 3 hours to do it. Power hikers will take about 2.5 hours. Because of the length of this route, it may be too long to take young kids in the backpack. Be sure to bring a lunch and water.

The Run: Weekend warriors love this run. It's a great workout because of the distance, and you get to enjoy the scenery along the way. After the grind up Kestrel, it's pretty easy going on the Freeway. Watch your footing on the way down Hulls because of rocks, sand and a few boulders. – SS

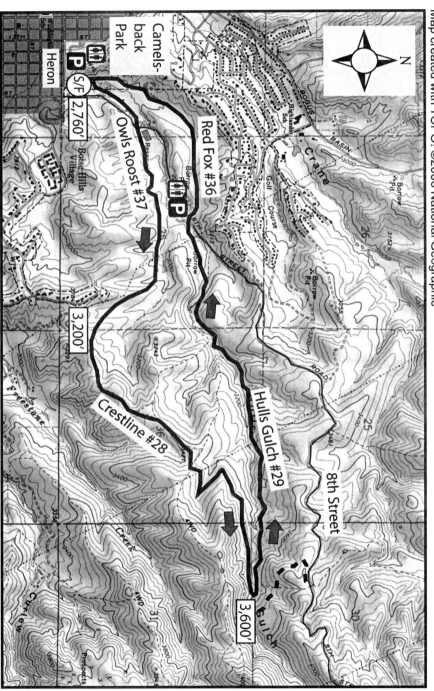

Map created with TOPO! ©2006 National Geographic

#34 Military Reserve Double Ridge Loop

Location: East Boise Foothills
Difficulty: Moderate, with short
strenuous pitches
Distance: 3.7 miles
Tread: Singletrack
Hiking time: 1:30
Running time: 50 minutes
Vertical gain/loss: 570 feet
Watch out for: Mountain bikers
and other trail users
Water: Dependable in pond near
trailhead; seasonal in Cottonwood
Creek

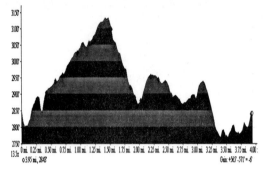

Season: March - October; winter use may be feasible when trails are frozen.

Getting there: From downtown Boise, take State Street east to Fort Street, and then turn left on Reserve Street. Go a half mile and turn left on Mountain Cove Road. Follow Mountain Cove to a right-hand corner and proceed 100 yards to the trailhead. The hike/run starts here.

General notes: The Military Reserve Double Ridge Loop provides a great workout suitable for a quick lunchtime run or an after-work hike. It also features a nice tour of the Central Ridge and Eagle Ridge areas in Military Reserve Park. Pay attention to dog regulations and please clean up after your pet. Bags are stocked at the trailhead.
Directions: Head up Toll Road Trail #27A, cross the creek, and turn left on Central Ridge Trail #22. Climb the steep but short grade that switchbacks to the Central Ridge, providing a great view in a matter of minutes. Bear left at the junction with Trail #22A to take a moderate route to the ridgetop. Turn right on Trail #20 at mile 1.1 and you'll reach the ridgetop at mile 1.4. Take a breather and enjoy the view. Take Ridge Crest Trail #20 down the hill to the next junction. Turn left, cross the creek, and take another left on Eagle Ridge #25. It's a steep abrupt climb up to the top of the ridge, but once you're on top, it's pretty flat. Follow Eagle Ridge trail to the radio tower, go straight on pavement for a moment, and then veer left to Eagle Ridge Loop Trail #25A. Do the loop (.5 miles), and then head down the paved road again, and take an immediate left to Eagle Rock. Go left and follow the Pond Trail to the base of the mountain. Take an immediate right and cruise toward the pond. Bear left by the pumphouse, and continue on the concrete apron on the right side of the creek to the Black Forest Trail. Follow the trail to the second junction, turn left and return to the trailhead.

The Hike: This is a great quick getaway hike that provides nice views and some decent exercise, close to town.
The Run: This running route is just about perfect for the weekend warrior. To mix things up, try reversing the route next time you do it. – SS

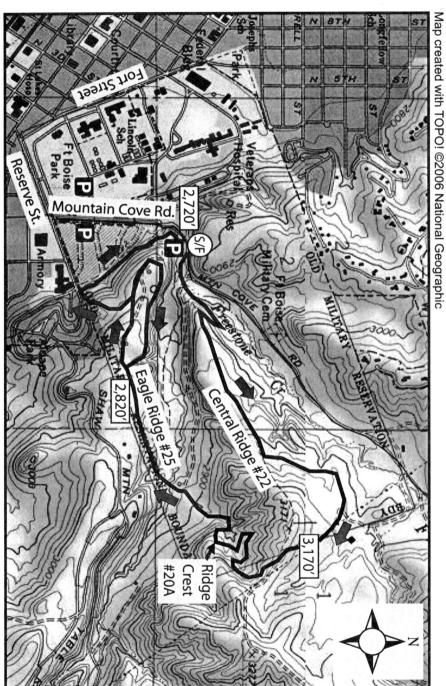

Map created with TOPO! ©2006 National Geographic

#35 Military Reserve Two Coyote Loop

Location: East Boise Foothills
Difficulty: Moderate, with short strenuous pitches
Distance: 6.5 miles
Tread: Singletrack, dirt road
Hiking time: 2:30
Running time: 1:15
Vertical gain/loss: 705 feet
Watch out for: Mountain bikers, other trail users
Water: Dependable in pond near trailhead; seasonal in Freestone Creek

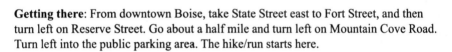

Season: March - October; winter use may be feasible when trails are frozen.

Getting there: From downtown Boise, take State Street east to Fort Street, and then turn left on Reserve Street. Go about a half mile and turn left on Mountain Cove Road. Turn left into the public parking area. The hike/run starts here.

General notes: The Two Coyote Loop was named by the Boise Bs after they saw two different coyotes chasing mice in the grassy meadows along Bucktail Trail. The route starts on a mellow note, climbing very gradually along Freestone Creek, and then the grade increases as you scale Bucktail and part of Shane's. After that, it's a fun singletrack descent into Freestone Creek, and a wide-open downhill on a dirt road back to the Freestone singletrack. Watch for coyotes, deer, fox and hawks.

Directions: Cross Mountain Cove Road and take an immediate left on the wide dirt trail paralleling the paved road. Rejoin the road around the corner. Turn right at the Toll Road Trailhead, cross the creek, and take an immediate left on Freestone Creek Trail #22B. Follow the sinewy singletrack for a mile to Trail #20. Turn right and climb an abrupt hill to Bucktail Trail #20A. Peel left and enjoy the gradual winding climb on Bucktail for over a mile to Shane's junction. Turn left and follow Shane's #26A up a fairly steep grade to the Trail #26/#26A junction. Go left on #26 and descend to Freestone Creek alongside tall bitterbrush. Cross the creek, climb a short steep pitch and then the trail dumps out on a dirt road. Bear left on the road. It's slightly downhill for a bit, and then steeper downhill as it returns to the police firing range area. Pick up the Freestone Creek Trail by the Trail #20 junction and retrace your steps to the start.

The Hike: This is a cool variation to the Central Ridge - Bucktail Loop, with 2 miles of additional mileage afforded by the link to Shane's Trail and Trail #26.

The Run: This is a substantial 1-hour-plus run that climbs very gradually at the start and gets progressively steeper toward the top of the loop. There's plenty of fun, winding singletrack along the route to enjoy. Watch your footing on the road downhill.
– Boise Bs and SS

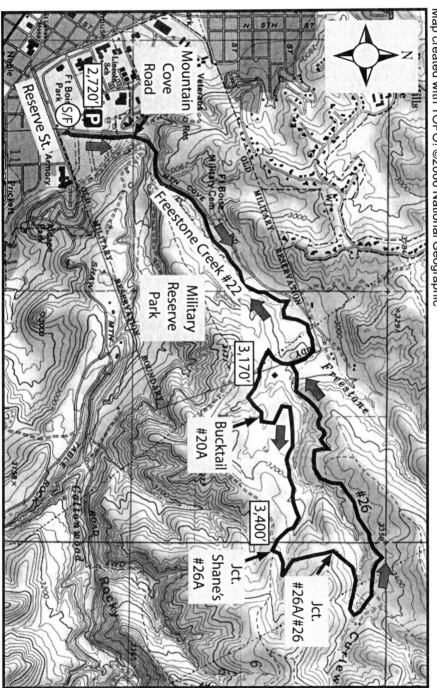

#36 Shane's Loop

Location: East Boise Foothills
Difficulty: Moderate
Distance: 4.5 miles
Tread: Dirt road, singletrack
Hiking time: 1:30
Running time: 50 minutes
Vertical gain/loss: 729 feet
Watch out for: Mountain bikers
and speeding vehicles on Rocky
Canyon Road

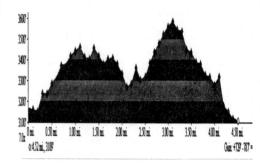

Water: Seasonal in Cottonwood
Creek along Rocky Canyon Road; dry on Shane's
Season: March - October; winter use may be feasible when trails are frozen.

Getting there: From downtown Boise, take State Street east to Fort Street, and then turn left on Reserve Street. Go straight on Reserve to a sharp right-hand bend and go uphill on Shaw Mountain Road to a 3-way junction at the top of the hill with Table Rock Road and Rocky Canyon Road. Go left on Rocky Canyon and proceed about 2 miles to the parking area at the end of the pavement. The hike/run starts here.

General notes: Shane's Loop is a sweet singletrack hike/run close to Boise. It's a double pull, climbing up to the initial first grade to the top of Curlew Ridge, and then a second climb to Shane's Summit. Folks can shorten the route by a mile by parking in a small pullout next to the Shane's Trailhead on Rocky Canyon Road. When going up Rocky Canyon road, watch out for speeding vehicles, ATVs, motorcycles and mountain bikes. Watch for wildlife on the trail. Shane's Trail is named for the late Shane Erickson, a guy who was very active in mountain bike projects for SWIMBA.

Directions: Head up Rocky Canyon Road and climb .6 miles on the dirt road to Shane's Trailhead #26A on the left side of the road. Water your dog before leaving Cottonwood Creek. Climb several switchbacks on Shane's to the top of Curlew Ridge. Here, you'll come to a junction. Go left to do it clockwise. Now it's a nice contour cruise across the grassy foothills to the west. The trail bends left and drops down to the Bucktail Trail junction at mile 2. Bear right and climb a strenuous pull up the Shane's grade. Ignore a left-hand junction for Trail #26, bear right and keep climbing. You'll reach the Shane's Summit at Mile 3. Take a moment to enjoy the view. Drop down Trail #26A, bear left at the loop junction, and return to the trailhead.

The Hike: This is a cool hike close to town that provides great views of the city.

The Run: This route works great for a lunchtime or after-work workout. It's a tough climb up to Curlew Ridge and a strenuous pull to Shane's Summit, but many other parts of the loop are a fun and easy singletrack cruise. – SS

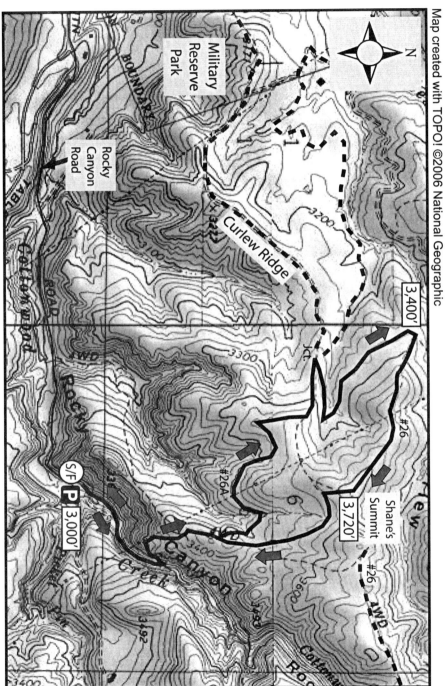

Map created with TOPO! ©2006 National Geographic

Military
Reserve
Park

Rocky
Canyon
Road

Curlew Ridge

3,400'

#26

Shane's
Summit

3,720'

#26A

S/F
P 3,000'

Canyon

Creek

#26 4WD

Jct.

#37 Orchard Gulch - 5 Mile Creek Loop

Location: East Boise Foothills
Difficulty: Moderate to strenuous
Distance: 5.35 miles
Tread: Singletrack, dirt road
Hiking time: 2:30
Running time: 1:10
Vertical gain/loss: 1,149 feet
Watch out for: Wildlife, mountain
bikers and speeding vehicles
Water: Seasonal in Orchard Gulch;
dependable in Five Mile Creek
Season: March - October

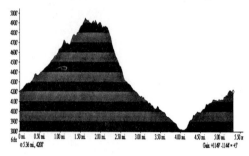

Getting there: From downtown Boise, take E. State Street to Reserve Street. Turn left on Reserve and follow it to a sharp right-hand bend. Turn right and now you're on Shaw Mountain Road. Drive up Shaw Mountain 2 miles to the top of the hill. At a 3-way junction, turn left on Rocky Canyon Road and follow that 5 miles to the Trail #7 trailhead in Orchard Gulch. The hike/run starts here.

General notes: This is a nice off-the-beaten-track venue for a loop hike/run near Rocky Canyon Road. Both Orchard Gulch and Five Mile Creek are nice, quiet draws with large cottonwood trees and cool spots for a picnic. It's a fairly strenuous climb up Orchard Gulch, but once you're on top, it's pretty easy-going from there. Watch for elk, deer, fox and hawks. Access in this area was made possible by the Foothills levy.

Directions: Head up Trail #7 into Orchard Gulch. You'll climb along the creek for .9 miles until the trail crosses the creek and climbs a steep grade to the ridgetop and intersects with a two-track road. Ignore the junction with an old fire-break road that climbs abruptly up the ridge, and bear left on the two-track and follow it as it contours over to a fork of Five Mile Creek. You'll notice that the two-track continues to climb toward the Boise Ridge. Turn left at the fork and descend into Five Mile Creek. Cross the creek (thick brush), and go left on the two-track heading down Five Mile back to Rocky Canyon Road. Once at the road, turn left and climb back to the trailhead.

The Hike: This is a great secluded hike that doesn't get much use. The creek settings are nice and full of songbirds, and then the ridge between Orchard Gulch and Five Mile Creek provides great views.

The Run: Pace yourself in the beginning as you climb an increasingly steep grade up Orchard Gulch to the ridge above it. Once on top, it's a nice cruise. Watch your footing on the descent into Five Mile Ceek, and then it's a fun moderate downhill along the creek. After that, alas, you have to climb back to the trailhead – it's 1.2 miles over 375 vertical feet back to the start. – SS

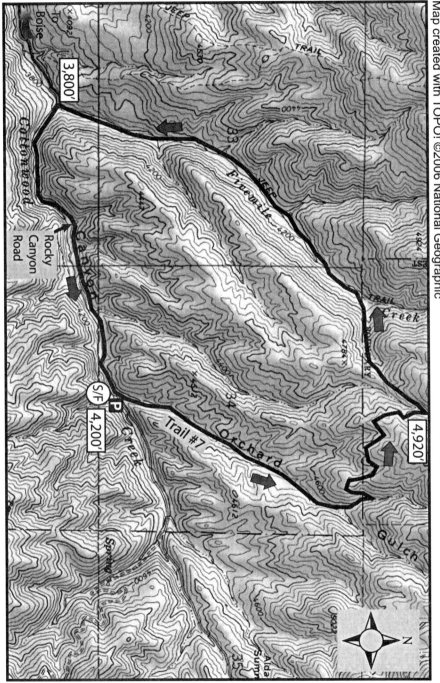

Map created with TOPO! ©2006 National Geographic

#38 Explore Turner Gulch

Location: Foothills above Lucky
Peak Reservoir, east of Boise
Difficulty: Moderate
Distance: 4.35 miles
Tread: Singletrack
Hiking time: 2+ hours
Running time: NA
Vertical gain/loss: 1,160 feet
Watch out for: Wildlife
Water: Seasonal in Turner Gulch
Season: April - October; winter use
may be feasible when trails are frozen

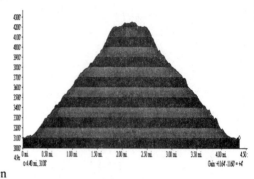

Getting there: From the intersection of Broadway and Warm Springs Avenue in east
Boise, go east on Warm Springs to Idaho 21. Turn left and follow Idaho 21 to the top
of Lucky Peak Dam. Turn right and follow the paved road over the dam to the Turner
Gulch boat ramp and parking area. The hike/run starts here.

General notes: This is a neat hike close to Boise that features cool rock formations as
you climb into the gulch. It's fun scrambling around on the rocks in the creek bottom,
taking one of several paths up the creek. This route isn't suitable for running because
of the rocky route and poor footing. It's
probably best to hike this in the spring
before July, and then later in the fall in
September and October.

Directions: Head out of the southeast
corner of the parking area and pick up
the major trail that heads for Turner
Gulch. The trail goes downhill to the
bottom of the gulch. Pass through a
small gate, used for cattle grazing.
Continue hiking up the trail. It's about a
mile up the gulch to a point where the
rock formations get interesting. In the second mile, big rock formations surround the
bottom of the gulch, while you scramble up the trail on each side of the creek. Take a
moment to enjoy the scenery. After 2 miles, you will have climbed more than 1,000
feet, and the gulch forks. There is a faint trail up either fork. You may wish to turn
around here. The left fork provides the quickest way toward the top of the canyon, but
by then, you'll run into private land. Ditto with the right fork. Return to the start.

The Hike: This a good hike for young kids, the dog, kids in a backpack, whatever. It's
kind of a steep climb, but since it's a short hike, it's not very strenuous. Take your time
and enjoy it.– SS

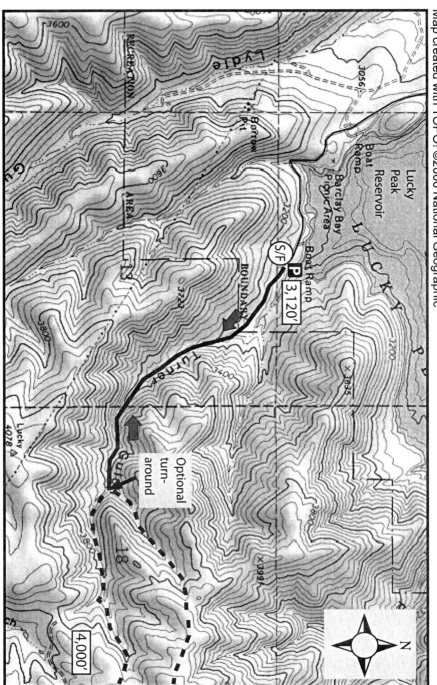

#39 Bogus Basin Contour Special

Location: Bogus Basin Resort
Difficulty: Moderate to strenuous
Distance: 5.75 miles
Tread: Singletrack; dirt road;
Hiking time: 2:30
Running time: 1:10
Vertical gain/loss: 1,497 feet
Watch out for: Wildlife,
wildflowers, other trail users
Water: Dry route unless the lodge is
open or a water spigot is available.
Season: June - October

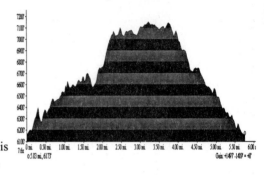

Getting there: From downtown Boise, take Harrison Boulevard north to the intersection of Bogus Basin Road and Hill Road. Go straight (north) on Bogus Basin road for approximately 18 miles to the lower lodge. The hike/run starts here.

General remarks: This is a sweet hike/run on several of Bogus Basin's new trails and existing trails that circumnavigate the whole ski mountain. It's pretty moderate climbing on the new Deer Point Trail #91, and then there are some short steep sections at the beginning of Elk Meadows. But after that, it's more up on the level as you circle the mountain. By the time you reach the top of Morning Star Chairlift, it's all downhill back to the lower lodge. When it's hot in July, it's a perfect time to go to Bogus where the temperatures can be 10-20 degrees cooler. Pack plenty of water and food.

Directions: Locate the bottom of Deer Point Trail #91 next to the Deer Point Express lift. Begin a gradual climb on the trail for almost two miles to the Bogus ridge, north of the Showcase Chairlift. This is all new trail, and it's beautiful. At the ridge, cross the road and pick up Elk Meadows Trail #94. It's steep for a short bit climbing through sage and timber and then it gets more gradual by the top of Nugget. Follow Elk Meadows around the backside of Bogus as it winds along the upper tier of the mountain. Elk Meadows dumps out on a cat track. Keep going west on the two-track dirt road around to the backside of Chair #3. Take a side trip to the top of Shafer Butte for the best view (optional). Stay on the dirt road and it eventually turns into Lodge Trail. It wraps around to Morning Star lift on a slight downhill. Turn left on Sunshine Trail, which dissolves into a flower-bordered singletrack. Then it intersects with Shindig and descends to the bottom of Showcase Chair. Go downhill to the lodge.

The Hike: This is a really nice hike for just about any skill level. Children under 8 might have a hard time doing the whole thing.

The Run: Escape the heat in Boise and enjoy a really nice cruise through the woods. To mix things up, you might try the loop in reverse direction next time.

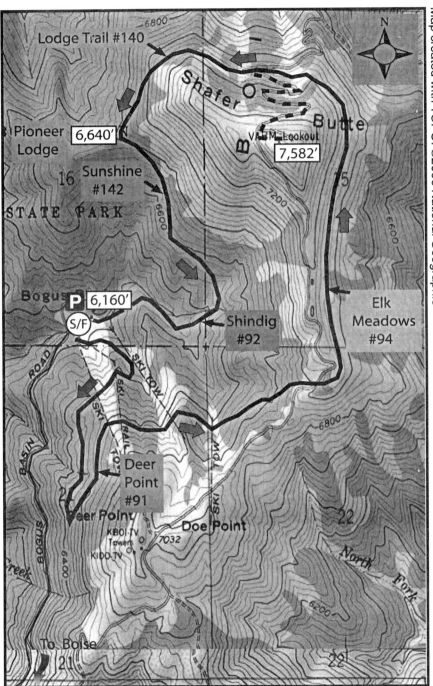

#40 Mores Mountain Loop

Location: Shafer Butte Picnic Area
Difficulty: Moderate to strenuous
Distance: 4.25 miles
Tread: Singletrack; dirt road
Hiking time: 1:45
Running time: 50 minutes
Vertical gain/loss: 1,000 feet
Watch out for: Wildlife,
wildflowers, other trail users
Water: Public spigot at the picnic
area during the summer season;
isolated mountain springs
Season: June - October

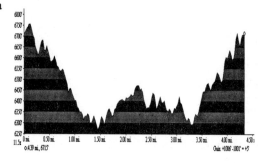

Getting there: From downtown Boise, take Harrison Boulevard north to the intersection of Bogus Basin Road and Hill Road. Drive up Bogus Basin Road to the lower lodge. Keep going straight on the Boise Ridge Road for another 2.5 miles to a right-hand turn for the Shafer Butte Picnic Area. Turn right and proceed to the picnic area. The hike/run starts here.

General notes: This is a nice loop that's great for nearly all abilities. Couples with small children can tag team the kids while one parent does the big loop, and the other plays with the kids. The route begins with a fun singletrack descent to the Boise Ridge Road, and then it contours and climbs back to the picnic area. The loop affords great views of the Sawtooths and the Boise National Forest off to the east. Wildflowers bloom big-time up here in July.

Directions: To begin, pick up the Mores Mountain singletrack next to the Mores Mountain Interpretive Trail, bear right and follow the trail downhill along the east slope of Mores Mountain. Trail #190 rolls up and down for 1.5 miles to the Boise Ridge Road. Turn left and follow the ridge road another 1.75 miles to the picnic area turnoff. Now it's a steep grade for about a mile back to the start.
Mores Mountain Summit Trail: As an alternative, take a short hike to the top of the mountain from the picnic area. Go left on the marked Mores Mountain Trail at the trailhead, and climb .75 miles and 400 vertical feet to the top. It's a great hike for kids.

The Hike: Bring a lunch, a camera and a wildflower guide and enjoy your surroundings as you circumnavigate Mores Mountain. When the weather gets hot in Boise, this a great place to beat the heat.

The Run: It starts out easy with a downhill (watch your footing), and it's a pretty easy cruise on the Boise Ridge Road, and then a tough pull back to the picnic area. It's a nice compact workout in a forest environment. – SS and Lynette McDougal

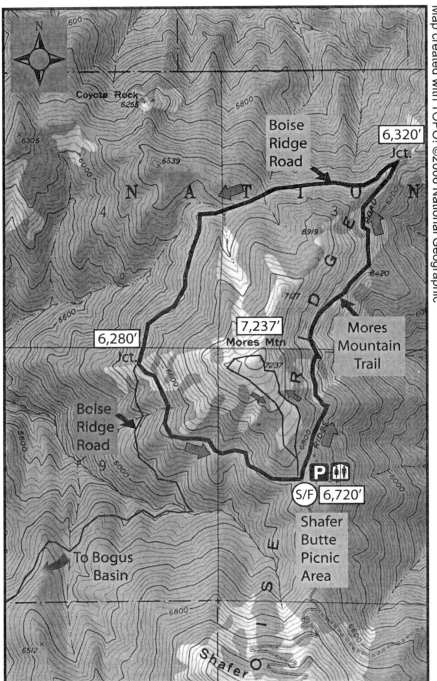

N

Coyote Rock
6255

Boise
Ridge
Road

6,320′
Jct.

Mores
Mountain
Trail

6,280′
Jct.

7,237′
Mores Mtn

Boise
Ridge
Road

P

S/F 6,720′

Shafer
Butte
Picnic
Area

To Bogus
Basin

Shafer

#41 Idaho City - Charcoal Gulch Loop

Location: Idaho City
Difficulty: Moderate
Distance: Charcoal Gulch out and back, 4 miles; Long loop, 6.5 miles
Tread: Dirt road, singletrack
Hiking time: Charcoal Gulch, 2 hours; Long loop, 2.5-3 hours
Running time: Charcoal Gulch, 40 minutes; Long loop, 1 hour
Vertical loss/gain: 1,100 feet
Watch out for: Motor vehicles, ATVs, other trail users
Water: Dependable in Charcoal Gulch
Season: May - October

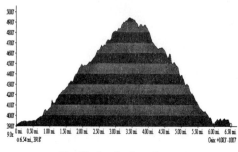

Profile for the long loop

Getting there: From Boise, take Idaho 21 east to Idaho City. Turn left on Main Street. Follow it several blocks to the junction with Bear Run Road and Centerville Road. Turn left on the Centerville Road (USFS Road #307) and follow that for .25 miles to Buena Vista Road on the left. Turn left and follow Buena Vista, past the Idaho City Airport, to the parking area and trailhead. The hike/run starts here.

General notes: Hikers/runners have several options to consider for this route. For hikers, I recommend going out and back on the Charcoal Gulch Trail (2 miles to the top), because the Centerville Road is not necessarily a pleasant place to walk – it's got a fair amount of traffic, the road is wide, and it's dusty in the hot summer. For runners, I recommend doing the full loop because it's worth putting up with the negatives to get the extra mileage. Be sure to pack plenty of water, snacks or a lunch to enjoy your time in Charcoal Gulch. It's a cool, forested creek environment.

Directions: **Charcoal Gulch out and back**: Head west out of the parking lot and take the ATV trail along the base of the mountain for a half mile to the junction with Charcoal Gulch Trail. Turn right and climb Charcoal Gulch 1.5 miles to the top. Take a break on top and retrace your steps to the trailhead. **Long loop**: Take Buena Vista Road back to the Centerville Road. Go left and climb #307 3.5 miles to the top. You'll see a sign on the left for the road to the Landfill, near the junction with USFS Road #311. Head for the Landfill, and peel left on the Charcoal Gulch trail. There are diamond markers on the trees for cross-country skiing. It's 2 miles down Charcoal Gulch. You'll cross the creek a couple times. Near the bottom, turn left at a T-junction with an ATV trail. Go left to the trailhead.

The Hike: It's 1,000 feet of climbing to the top. Take your time and enjoy it.
The Run: It's kind of a yin-yang situation because of the nasty dusty climb at the start of the run, but it all pays off on the nice downhill in Charcoal Gulch. – SS

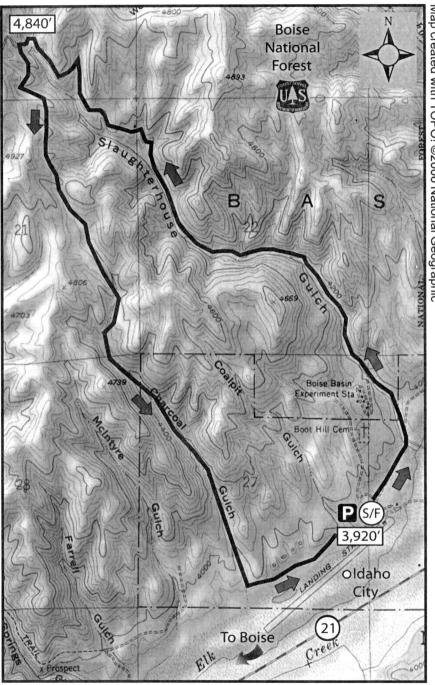

4,840'

Boise
National
Forest

N

Map created with TOPO! ©2006 National Geographic

Slaughterhouse

B   A   S

Gulch

Coalpit

Boise Basin
Experiment Sta

Charcoal

Boot Hill Cem

McIntyre

Gulch

Gulch

Gulch

Farrell

P (S/F)
3,920'

LANDING ST

Oldaho
City

To Boise   21

Gulch   Creek

Elk

Prospect

SPRINGS TRAIL

113

#42 Banner Ridge - Alpine - Elkhorn Loop

Location: Boise National Forest NE of Idaho City
Difficulty: Moderate to strenuous
Distance: 7.5 miles
Tread: 4WD dirt road, grassy two-track
Hiking time: 3 hours
Running time: 1:10 minutes
Vertical loss/gain: 958 feet
Watch out for: Wildlife; other trail users
Water: Small creeks and seeps; otherwise dry
Season: May - November

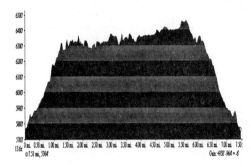

Getting there: From Boise, take Idaho 21 east to Idaho City. Continue east on Idaho 21 past Mores Creek Summit, Whoop-em-up Campground, and Gold Fork to a right-hand turn for Banner Ridge Park 'n Ski area. The hike/run starts here.

General notes: The ideal way to do this route is to rent the Banner Ridge yurt and do some hiking or trail running while you're hanging out with friends. Banner Ridge road starts out at a very steep clip, but once you turn off on the Alpine Trail, it's a really enjoyable, shady, gentle uphill cruise to Elkhorn Trail, with more gentle climbing to the top of Banner Ridge. Bring plenty of water, snacks and a lunch to enjoy the setting. I've seen black bear and elk along this trail. To reserve the Banner Ridge or Elkhorn yurt, go to the Idaho Parks web site: http://parksandrecreation.idaho.gov

Directions: Head out of the parking area and climb .6 miles to the signed turnoff for Alpine Trail on the right. Alpine is a beautiful grassy two-track contour trail that gains elevation slowly and gradually. At mile 3.2, you'll reach the end of Alpine Trail at a T junction with Elkhorn Trail. Go left and climb to a junction with Cougar Trail. Bear left and keep going to the top of Banner Ridge (mile 5). Take a moment to enjoy the views and check out the yurt. Go left on the Banner Ridge road and descend to the trailhead. It's a gradual uphill at first, and then a major plunge – you lose the last 750 feet of elevation in 1.5 miles. Watch out for deep ruts on the road.

The Hike: This is a good day's hike that may be suitable for kids 8 and over. It may be too long for babies in a backpack. Take your time and watch for wildlife.

The Run: This is a nice shady running route in the woods at about 6,000 feet elevation – a good getaway when it gets hot in the Treasure Valley. The climb on the Alpine Trail is especially sweet. – SS

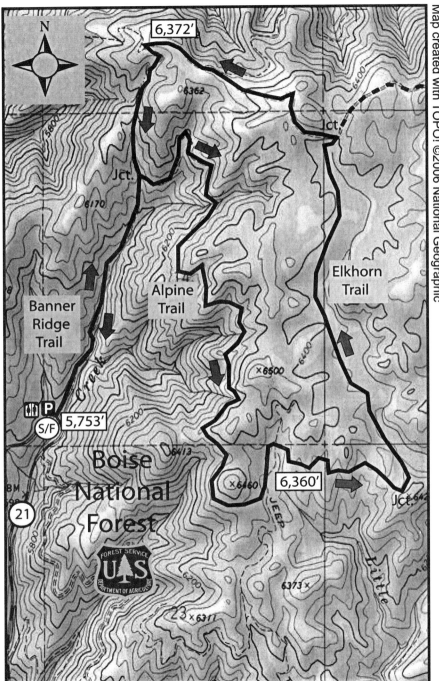

#43 Station Creek Loops

Location: Garden Valley
Difficulty: Easy to moderate
Distance: 3.5-mile short loop;
4.3-mile long loop
Tread: Nice, narrow singletrack
Hiking time: Short loop: 50-60
minutes; Long loop: 2+ hours at
leisurely pace
Running time: Short loop: 30
minutes; Long loop 1.5 hours
Vertical gain: 1,300 feet

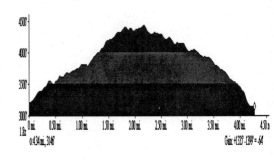

Watch out for: Interesting animal tracks: Deer, elk, coyote
Season: Late April - October

Getting there: Take Idaho 55 North to Banks. Turn right on the Banks to Lowman Highway and follow that to Garden Valley Ranger Station, east of Garden Valley. A primitive road to the Station Creek Trailhead peels off the north side of the highway. The hike/run starts here.

General notes: Station Creek is an easy-going trail on a rounded ridge that climbs to some beautiful viewpoints a thousand feet above the valley. The trail winds through a winter big game range, so you're likely to see critters. Be sure to keep your dog in control. It's also a great hike for carrying infants in the backpack or for young energetic kids age 5+. The trail climbs at a very reasonable grade all of the way.

Directions: Head up Station Creek Trail and enjoy the shady pine-bordered trail. After 1 mile, the trail winds out of the draw onto the ridge. It's another half-mile to the short-loop junction. At the trail junction sign, you can decide if you want to do the longer loop, or head back down the mountain. Continuing on, it's another half mile or so to the top of the trail (mile 2.1), where you'll see a sign for a trail going back to the Alder Creek Bridge. Take the left fork and follow the singletrack on a series of ridges back toward the highway. A mile from the top, the trail becomes sketchy and fizzles. Even so, it's easy to see the way down on an open ridge. Pick your route down to the highway and the silver bridge.

The Hike: Take your time and enjoy the views. Potential side trip: Go right at the summit junction and hike over to Bald Mountain, where you can get a better view.

The Run: The short loop provides a quick workout, and the longer route offers more miles and cool cross-country terrain. Sturdy shoes would be a good idea for the long loop, as there are many opportunities for twisted ankles in the steeper areas. Still, it's pretty easy going on grassy ridge slopes. – SS

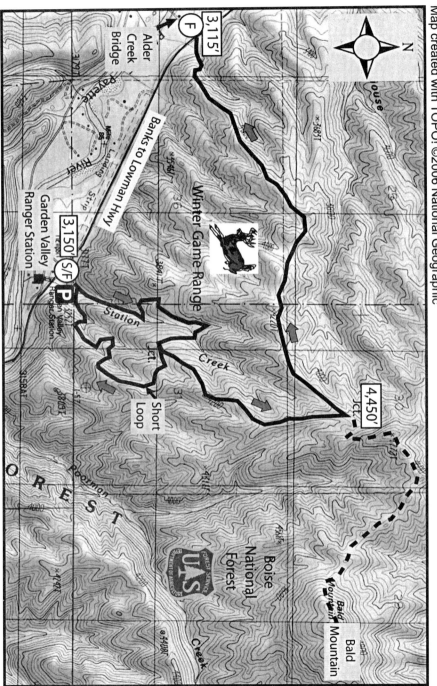

Map created with TOPO! ©2006 National Geographic

N

3,115'
F

Alder
Creek
Bridge

Payette

Banks to Lowman Hwy

Garden Valley
Ranger Station

3,150' S/F

P

Station

Jct.

Short
Loop

Creek

Winter Game Range

4,450' Jct.

Bald Mountain

F O R E S T

Boise
National
Forest

U/S FOREST SERVICE

Bald
Mountain

Creek

#44 Halverson Lake Loop

Location: Celebration Park in the
Snake River canyon, south of Nampa
Difficulty: Moderate
Distance: 5.8 miles
Tread: Dirt road, singletrack
Hiking time: 3 hours
Running time: 1:10
Vertical gain/loss: 106 feet
Keep an eye out for: Wildflowers,
birds of prey, other trail users
Water: Dependable in Snake River and Halverson Lakes
Season: Year-round

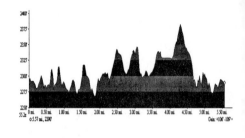

Getting there: From downtown Boise, hook up with I-184 west and head for Nampa. Take the Franklin Road exit in Nampa, and turn left. Follow Franklin to the junction with 11ᵗʰ Street. Turn right and take 11ᵗʰ into downtown Nampa. Follow signs for Idaho 45 south. Proceed to Walters Ferry at the Snake River. Just before the river crossing, turn left on Ferry Road. Follow Ferry to Hill Road. Go right on Hill to Sinker Road. Turn right on Sinker and proceed to Celebration Park. The hike/run starts here.

General remarks: This is a nice loop trail 45 minutes from Boise next to the Snake River. At the park, there are hundreds of boulders with petroglyph inscriptions – a great place for kids to wander around, climb on rocks and take pictures. The BLM has made the trail to Halverson Lake non-motorized, greatly improving the experience for hikers, runners, bikers and horseback riders. Bring water and a lunch to enjoy by the lake.

Directions: To begin, head out on a gravel road heading east to the official trailhead. Stay on the trail running along the bench above the Snake River. Ignore the left-hand forks for the return loops. At mile 2.3, go left and take the trail .5 miles to upper Halverson Lake. Take a break. On the way back, you'll see several trails winding around the rocks. Instead of heading back to the Snake River trail, hook up with a trail heading directly west that visits the second lake, slaloms around boulders, climbing uphill, and then it returns to the loop trail. You'll connect with the main trail at mile 4, and the trailhead at mile 5. Retrace your steps to the park.

The Hike: This is a great hike for anyone. Keep an eye out for horseback riders – this is a popular trail for equestrians. By parking at the actual trailhead, you can shave 1.6 miles off the route.

The Run: This is a fun and scenic running route adjacent to the Snake River. The route can be deep sand in places, so be prepared for slogging a bit here and there. Do this route in the spring or fall in the cooler weather. – SS

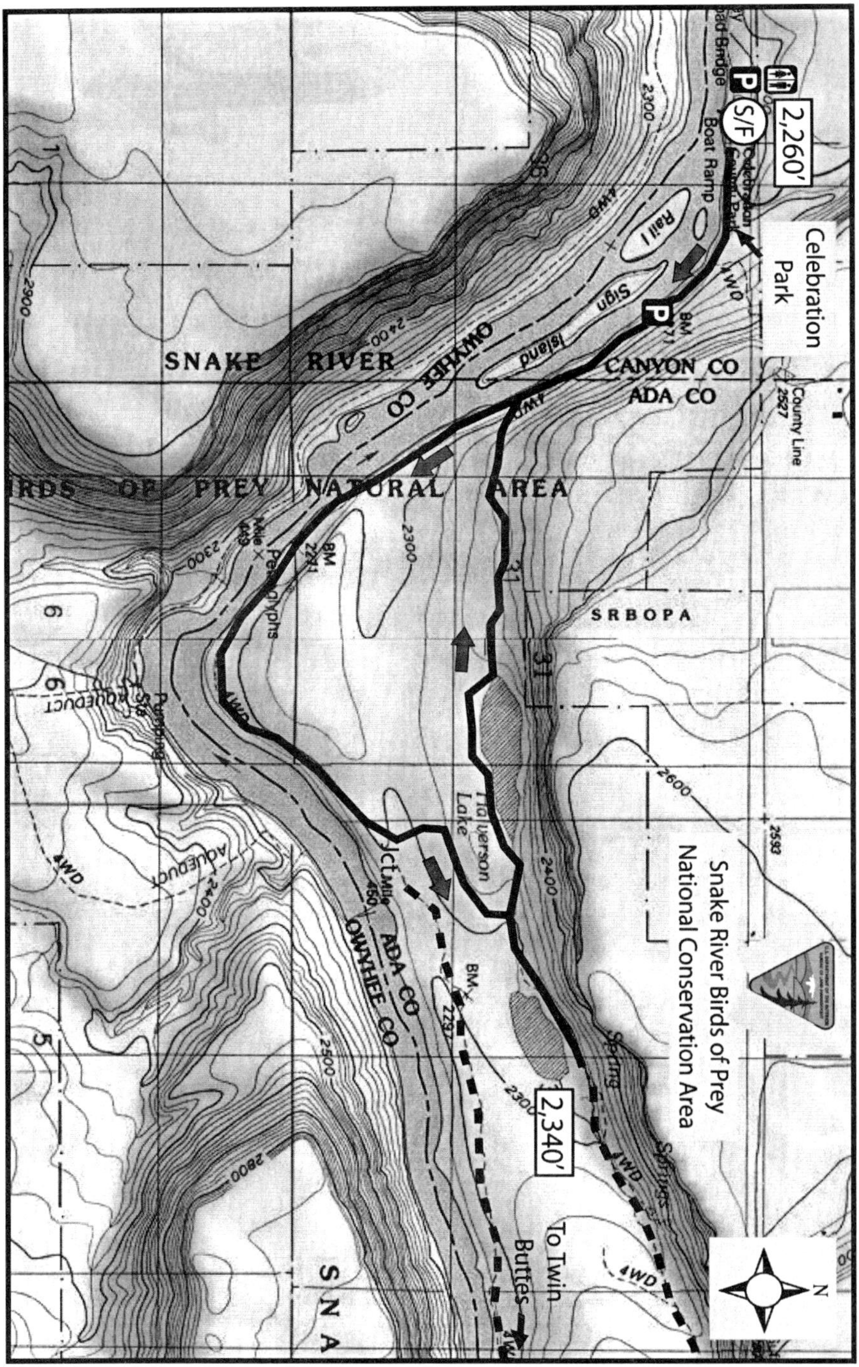

Map created with TOPO! ©2006 National Geographic

2,260'

Celebration Park

SNAKE RIVER

CANYON CO
ADA CO

County Line
2527

BIRDS OF PREY NATURAL AREA

SRBOPA

2593

OWYHEE CO

Halverson Lake

Snake River Birds of Prey
National Conservation Area

ADA CO
OWYHEE CO

2,340'

To Twin Buttes

N

#45 Wildcat Canyon Loop

Location: Owyhee Foothills, south-
west of Marsing
Difficulty: Moderate with short
strenuous pitches
Distance: 3.4 miles
Tread: Creek scramble and open
 ridge cruise
Hiking time: 2 hours
Running time: NA
Vertical gain/loss: 962/980 feet
Water: Seasonal
Season: April - October

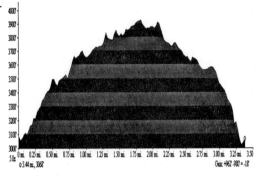

Getting there: From Boise, take I-84 west to the Idaho 55 South exit in Nampa.
Follow Idaho 55 south to Marsing. Proceed through Marsing and watch for a turnoff
for U.S. 95 west of town. Turn left on U.S. 95 South and head for Jordan Valley. The
unsigned right-hand turnoff is exactly six miles ahead. Go slow and watch for a dirt
road turnoff. A high-clearance 4WD vehicle is most suitable for this road. You'll drop
into a gully and then bear left at the first fork and follow the dirt road to the mouth of
the canyon. The hike starts here.

General notes: This is a nifty slot-canyon hike less than an hour from Boise. It's best
to wear shoes or sandals that can get wet. It's pretty easy going up Wildcat Canyon
creek, with beautiful, impressive rhyolite and basalt cliffs rising above you. There are a
number of spots where you'll need to scramble up a short steep ledge, and then it's
easy going again. After climbing up the draw two miles, you'll loop back on a parallel
draw that is more open, and then narrows down to a cliff, where you'll climb out of the
draw and hike to the ridge between the two canyons and cruise back to the trailhead.
This hike is good for kids 10 and over – they'll enjoy scambling up the creek and
checking out the rocks. Not recommended for dogs.

Directions/The Hike: Head out of the parking area and hike up Wildcat Canyon
Creek. You'll hike up the creek and scramble over a bunch of small ledges on your way
up the slot canyon. Take your time and enjoy the setting – it's only two miles to the top.
I rated the hike as moderate to strenuous because you still climb nearly 1,000 vertical
feet to the top end of Wildcat Canyon Creek. After you break out of the slot canyon,
you'll come to a fork. Follow the right fork and climb over a small hump to the next
draw. This may be a good place for a lunch break. Continuing on, turn right and hike
downhill in the draw a little over .5 miles, and you'll notice the canyon narrowing up:
There's a cliff ahead. Before that, bear right and climb up the slope to the top of the
ridge between the two draws. Cruise over to the cliff area to check it out from above.
Then scramble down the nose of the ridge back to the trailhead. – SS

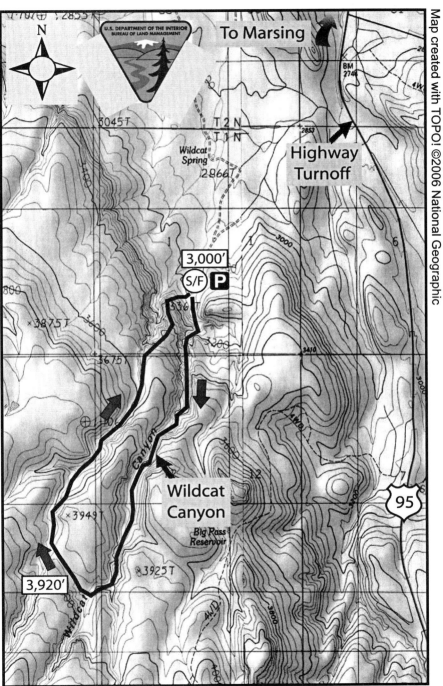

To Marsing

Highway Turnoff

3,000'

S/F P

Wildcat Canyon

95

3,920'

Map created with TOPO! ©2006 National Geographic

#46 Reynolds Creek Loop

Location: Owyhee Mountains,
south of Nampa
Difficulty: Moderate to
strenuous
Distance: 7.4 miles
Tread: Singletrack, dirt road
Hiking time: 3:30 hours

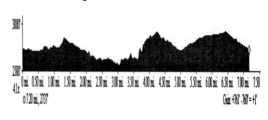

Running time: 1:10
Vertical gain/loss: 751 feet
Keep an eye out for: Wildlife, wildflowers, other trail users
Water: Dependable in Reynolds Creek; otherwise it's a dry route.
Season: March-November

Getting there: From downtown Boise, take I-184 west and head for Nampa. Take the Franklin Road exit (City Center) in Nampa, and turn left. Follow Franklin to the junction with 11th Street. Turn right and take 11th into downtown. Follow signs for Idaho 45 south. Take Idaho 45 to Walters Ferry at the Snake River and turn right on Idaho 78, heading for Marsing. In a couple miles, turn left on Wilson Creek Road. Proceed up the paved road until it turns to dirt and pull into a dirt parking area on the left. The hike/run starts here.

General notes: This is a great hike/run in the Owyhee foothills, about 45 minutes from Boise. The trail weaves through rock formations on the way over to Reynolds Creek, and then you hike/run on top of an old Chinese-built irrigation ditch high above the creek. The red rock canyon is spectacular. Bring a camera, plenty of water and a lunch.

Directions: To begin, pick up Trail #300 on the west side of the parking lot. Ignore trails branching off to the left in the first mile. At mile .9, you'll cross a road and continue on the singletrack. The trail climbs one last hill and then widens into a two-track and descends to a T-junction at a dirt road (mile 1.8). Go right and then left on Trail #410, a sandy wash going downhill towards Reynolds Creek. At mile 2.3, go right on Trail #310 and proceed for a half mile to a junction with Trail #600, the China Ditch trail. Go right and walk upstream along Reynolds Creek for a long mile. At a junction with Trails #510, #601 and #610, go right on #510 and climb out of the canyon. At mile 4, bear right at a Y junction and stay on #510 to BLM dirt road #37154. Go right and follow the road to the junction with Trail #400. Go left on #400 at mile 5.28 and head back to the trailhead. At the top of the first hill, you can either stay on Trail #400 or branch off on #300 to the right. Both ways return to the start.

The Hike: Even though the route is 7+ miles, the elevation gain is pretty minimal, so the hike may be suitable for kids 8 and over. My kids made it, but they were tired.
The Run: This is a great spot for a trail run, with cool rock formations, steep redrock walls and good footing most of the way. – SS

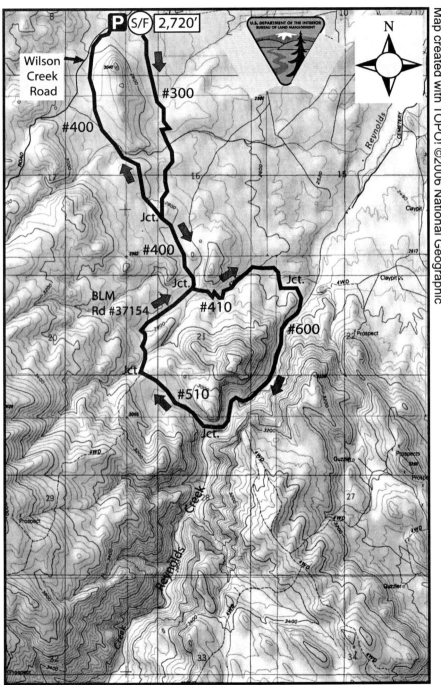

P S/F 2,720'

N

Wilson
Creek
Road

#300

#400

Jct.

#400

BLM
Rd #37154

Jct.

#410

Jct.

#600

Jct.

#510

Jct.

U.S. DEPARTMENT OF THE INTERIOR
BUREAU OF LAND MANAGEMENT

Reynolds Creek

#47 Leslie Gulch-Juniper Gulch Scramble

Location: Leslie Gulch in Oregon
Difficulty: Moderate to strenuous
Distance: 2 miles in Juniper Gulch;
5.5 miles to Yellow Jacket and back
Tread: No marked trail; sandy creek
bottom wash and rock hopping
Hiking Time: 2:30
Running Time: NA
Vertical gain/loss: 400 feet in
Juniper; 890 feet to the top
Watch out for: Snakes; flash floods
Water: Seasonal in Juniper Gulch
and Leslie Gulch; dependable in
Owyhee Reservoir
Season: March - October

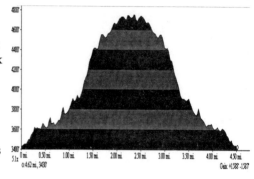

Getting there: From Nampa, follow Highway 55 south 18 miles to Marsing until you intersect U.S. 95. Turn left on U.S. 95 and drive 16 miles until you come to a BLM Leslie Gulch sign. Turn right on a gravel road and follow it for 22 miles, following Leslie Gulch signs. The Juniper Gulch Trailhead is marked on the right.

General notes: Leslie Gulch is a BLM recreation area with outstanding scenic features – redrock spires, buttes and hoodoos that harken images of southern Utah. Numerous side canyons with sheer rock walls and catacomb-like rock formations inspire exploration. Bring your camera. In lower Leslie Gulch near the Owyhee Reservoir boat ramp, 3.5 miles past Juniper Gulch, you will find a public rest room and camping area. Watch for wildlife: wild horses and bighorn sheep in particular.

Directions/The Hike: From the Juniper Gulch trailhead, follow a primitive trail about 100 yards north to the mouth of Juniper Gulch. Follow the winding creek bed for 1 mile. The volcanic tuff-rock walls close in on you almost immediately. As you hike, admire the interesting catacomb rock formations and side canyons. Strike a pose in the many Swiss cheese-like formations. At mile 1, the canyon starts to open up into sagebrush hills. If you want a leisurely hike, just turn around and scramble 1 mile back down the creekbed to your car. If you're game for a good view of the entire Leslie Gulch area, continue climbing up the drainage and look to the left up the steep hillside to find a way to reach the high ridge. Try to stay out in the open away from the rock cliffs. Once on top of the ridge, hike south to a high point called "The Yellow Jacket." The views are spectacular. **Do not be tempted** to take the seemingly direct route off the south face of the Yellow Jacket to your vehicle 1,300 feet below. There are no safe routes down without climbing gear. Return the same way you came, or hike east and then south along the high ridge until you end up on the main Leslie Gulch road. If you take that route, you will end up a couple miles below where your car is parked.
– Leo Hennessy and SS

124

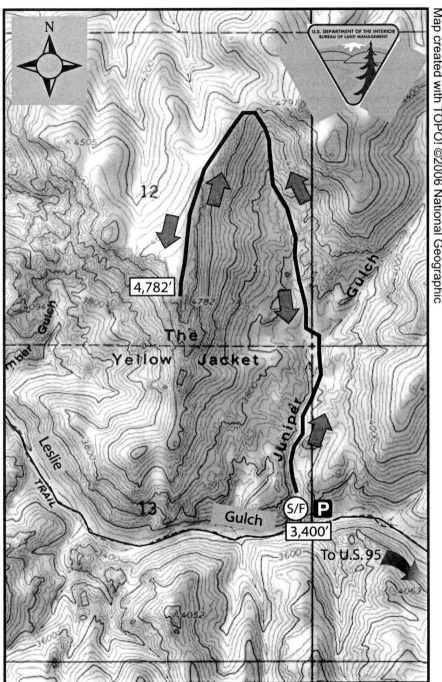

Strenuous Mountain Trails

48. Hillside to the Hollow (p. 128)
49. Corrals to Corrals (p. 130)
50. Crestline - Sidewinder Loop (p. 132)
51. Hulls - Sidewinder Loop (p. 134)
52. Hulls Gulch Interpretive Trail (p. 136)
53. Hulls - Bob's Loop (p. 138)
54. Jumpin' Jeepers Figure 8 Loop (p. 140)
55. Military Reserve to Sidewinder Loop (p. 142)
56. Three Bears Loop (p. 144)
57. Foothills on the Rocks (p. 146)
58. Candyland Table Rock Loop (p. 148)
59-60. Squaw Creek Loops (p. 150)
61. Twin Peaks at Bogus Basin Loop (p. 152)
62. Cottonwood Creek out and back (p. 154)
63. Pilot Peak out and back (p. 156)
64. Sunset Mountain Lookout out and back (p. 158)
65. Zimmer Creek Loop (p. 160)
66. Tripod Peak out and back (p. 162)
67. One Spoon Steepness (p. 164)
68. Snake River Petroglyph Tour (p. 166)

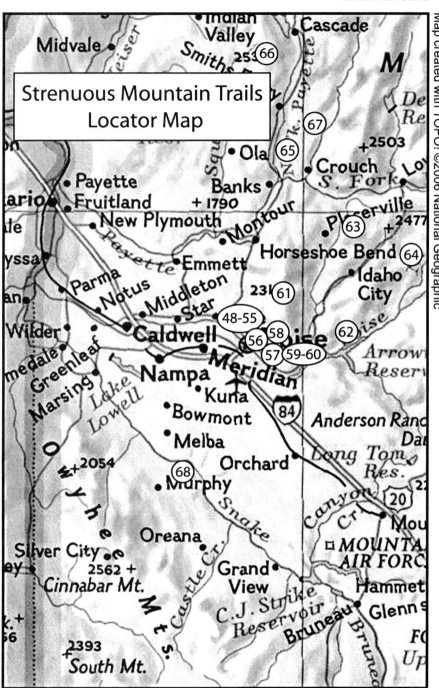

Strenuous Mountain Trails Locator Map

#48 Hillside to the Hollow

Location: Boise Foothills
Difficulty: Strenuous, with moderate pitches
Distance: 5.25 miles
Tread: Singletrack
Hiking time: 2+ hours
Running time: 1:10
Vertical gain/loss: 990 feet
Watch out for: Mountain bikers and other trail users.
Water: None

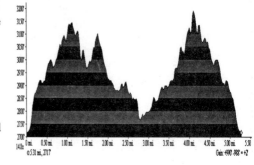

Season: March - October; winter use may be feasible when trails are frozen

Getting there: Follow Hill Road west of Bogus Basin Road to 36th Street. Turn right into Hillside Junior High. Go to the back of the school parking lot. Park. The hike/run starts here. **Alternative access**: An excellent trailhead and parking area are located next to the entrance to Heathwise off of Bogus Basin Road.

General notes: The route described here provides a tour of the area from Hillside Junior High to the bottom of Harrison Hollow and back. As one can see from the map, many other trail combinations are possible. **Note: The trails in this area are located entirely on private land (at press time) and could be subject to closure, re-route or other changes**. See www.hillsidetothehollow.org for more information.

Directions: Head up the steep trail to the northeast of the Hillside Jr. High tennis courts and follow it up the nose of the ridge. In .25 miles, you'll come to a trail junction. Go slightly to the left to follow the contour singletrack around the left side of the mountain for the most gentle approach (still strenuous) to the main ridge. Follow the ridge trail over the top of the ridge. It's 1.25 miles and 800 vertical feet to top. Continue east on the ridge and you'll come to a steep descent to a saddle before mile 2. Watch your step on the steeps. At the saddle junction, turn right and drop into Harrison Hollow. It's about 1 mile down to the trailhead by Healthwise. Turn around and head back up the gulch. You can climb the ridge on the right side of the gulch until a trail brings you back into the gulch. At the saddle junction, retrace your tracks or take a different trail back to Hillside Junior High.

The Hike: This is a strenuous but rewarding hike with great views of the valley. Many, shorter hikes are possible from neighborhood trailheads.

The Run: It's tough and strenuous – to say the least – to run this route. It's steep and anaerobic climbing, and then you recover on the more gentle grades. Take small steps on the climbs to maintain a doable pace on the steeps. – SS

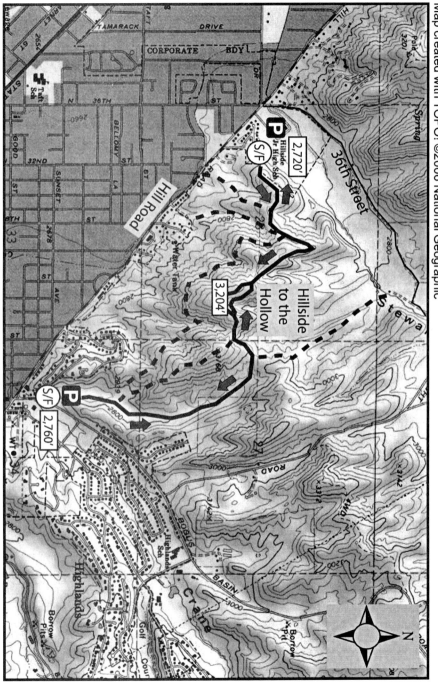

#49 Corrals to Corrals Loop

Location: Boise Central Foothills
Difficulty: Strenuous to gonzo
Distance: 12 miles
Tread: Singletrack, dirt road, sandy in places
Hiking time: 4-6 hours
Running time: 2:30
Vertical gain: 2,191 feet
Watch out for: Vehicles and motorcycles on 8th street; other trail users

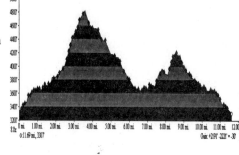

Water: Seasonal in Crane Creek adjacent to Corrals Trail
Season: March - October; winter use not feasible on upper portion of loop.

Getting there: From downtown Boise, take Harrison Boulevard north to the intersection of Bogus Basin Road and Hill Road. Go straight (north) on Bogus Basin road for about 3 miles to the dirt pullout/Corrals Trailhead. The hike/run starts here.

General notes: This is a double-pull hike/run that guarantees a hefty workout. You'll warm up climbing Corrals, and then the going gets tough going up Scott's to 8th Street. No matter how good of shape I'm in, this hill kicks my ass every time. After a steep downhill on 8th Street to the motorcycle parking lot, you'll descend on Trail #1 over to the backside of Corrals and get your butt kicked again on the steep climb to Corrals Summit. From there, it's all downhill. Be sure to pack plenty of food and water.

Directions: Head up Corrals Trail #31 to the green gate and pass through. Ignore the left-hand turn for Hard Guy by the corrals, and drop into a draw next to Crane Creek. The water along the trail for the next mile is the last you'll see for a long while. Once the trail switchbacks to Corrals Summit, the climbing gets steeper. At the first summit, turn left on Scott's Trail #32 and climb that nasty thing for 1.2 miles to 8th Street. Take a breather. Turn right and go down 8th Street 2.5 miles to the Trail #1 junction on the right across from the motorcycle parking lot entrance. No matter if you're hiking or running, you might want to run this section. It's steep! Go right on Trail #1 (step over steel barrier) and follow the trail around the corner. Ignore the left-hand fork with Bob's Trail and climb to Corrals Summit. It's 2.2 miles and 400 vertical feet of climbing to the top. The trail gets progressively steeper as you near the top. At Corrals Summit, turn left and return to the trailhead.

The Hike: Because of the challenging nature of this route, it's probably more appealing to a power-hiker than someone who wants pure scenery.
The Run: Only experienced and strong runners should attempt this route. It's possible to hike and run the loop to build endurance. People enjoy this double-pull loop because it puts their bodies to the test. Pace yourself. – Lynette McDougal and SS

Map created with TOPO! ©2006 National Geographic

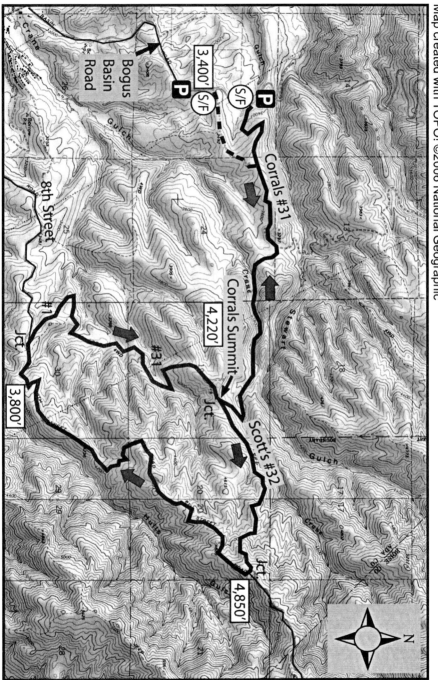

#50 Crestline - Sidewinder Loop

Location: Boise Central Foothills
Difficulty: Strenuous, with moderate pitches
Distance: 9 miles
Tread: Singletrack
Hiking time: 4 hours
Running time: 2 hours
Vertical gain/loss: 1,252 feet
Watch out for: Mountain bikers and dogs on the loose
Water: Seasonal in lower Hulls Gulch; plenty in Hulls Ponds near trailhead
Season: March - October; winter use may be feasible if trails are frozen.

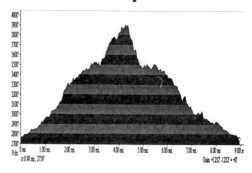

Getting there: From downtown Boise, take North 9th Street to a dead end parking area on the east edge of Camel's Back Park. The hike/run starts here. Parking also is available in the Camel's Back Park parking lot, near the junction of 13th and Heron.
General notes: After you've conquered the Freeway-Hulls Loop, it's time to up the ante and conquer the climb to the top of Sidewinder. Sidewinder starts out at a gradual uphill grade, and then it gets progressively steeper as you get near the top. It's a steep downhill on Trail #4 (watch your footing), and then a pretty moderate cruise down the Freeway to Red Cliffs (steep downhill pitches), and back to Camelsback.

Directions: Head up Red Fox Trail #31. Turn right at the first pond, and pick up Owls Roost Trail #37. Climb the gradual uphill trail, cross 8th Street and pickup Kestrel Trail #39A near the Hulls Gulch Interpretive Center. Climb Kestrel a half mile to Crestline Trail #28, commonly known as the Freeway. Turn left on the Freeway. It's mostly gradual climbing on the Freeway 1.3 miles to Sidewinder junction. Turn right and climb Sidewinder on the twisting trail with great views. Conserve energy as the trail gets steeper and you approach the Sidewinder Summit. You've traveled 4.5 miles and scaled 1,252 feet. Head down Trail #4 (steep!) to the Freeway, turn left and cruise on a slight downhill grade for a mile to Red Cliffs Trail #39. Bear right on Red Cliffs and enjoy the twisting steep downhill trail to Hulls Gulch. Bear left on Hulls and follow it to the parking area junction. Turn right, cross 8th Street, and take Red Fox Trail #36 back to the trailhead.

The Hike: This is a substantial foothills hike that provides a great tour of the central foothills trails. Be sure to bring plenty of food and water.

The Run: This is a pretty major run for the weekend warrior (9 miles over 2 hours). Take your time climbing up Kestrel and Sidewinder, these two trails are the steepest part of the route. Watch your footing descending Trail #4 and Red Cliffs (both can be rutted and sandy). – Boise Bs and SS

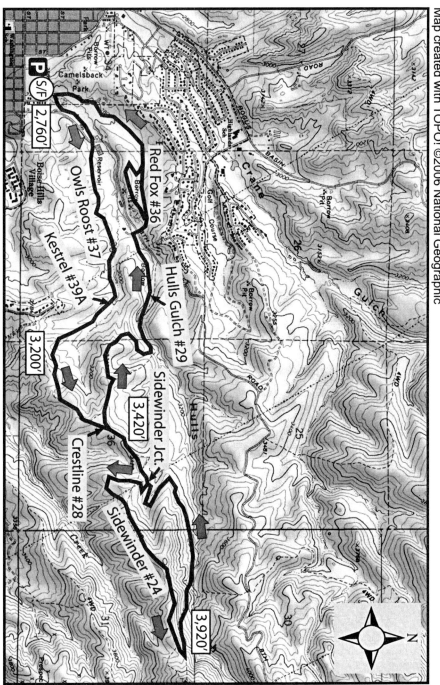

#5 I Hulls - Sidewinder Loop

Location: Boise Central Foothills
Difficulty: Strenuous, with
moderate pitches
Distance: 10.5 miles
Tread: Singletrack
Hiking time: 4+ hours
Running time: 2:15
Vertical gain/loss: 1,627 feet
Watch out for: Mountain bikers
and other trail users
Water: Seasonal in Hulls Gulch;

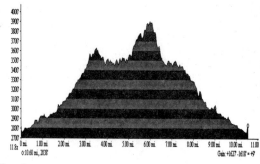

plenty in Hulls Ponds near the trailhead
Season: March - October; winter use may be feasible if trails are frozen

Getting there: From downtown Boise, take North 9th Street to a dead end parking area on the east edge of Camelsback Park. The hike/run starts here. Parking also is available in the Camelsback Park parking lot, near the junction of 13th and Heron.

General notes: Once you've mastered the Freeway - Sidewinder Loop, try this triple-pull special. It features a quick climb to Chickadee Ridge, and a continuous pull up Hulls Gulch, and another ascent up to Sidewinder Summit. After you finish this one, covering 10.5 miles and 1,627 vertical feet, you'll be ready for a beer or a hot tub – you've earned it. Watch your footing on the way down on Trail #4.

Directions: Head up Red Fox Trail #31. Climb the first abrupt hill and then take a right-hand turn on Chickadee Ridge #36A. Climb a couple switchbacks and cruise over to 8th Street. Go left after crossing 8th Street and head up Hulls Gulch Trail #29. You'll climb the beautiful creekside trail for 2+ miles to the Crestline-Hulls junction, which we call the "Living Room" due to the great conversations that occur there. Turn right, cross the creek and cruise down Crestline – "the Freeway." Pass the junction with Trail #4. It's less than a mile to Sidewinder Trail #24. Peel left on the fun twisting trail – it's 1.4 miles and 500+ feet of climbing to the top. Conserve energy. Take a moment to soak in the views at the summit. You've climbed 1,627 feet over 6.5 miles. Now it's all downhill. Head down Trail #4 (steep!) to Crestline, turn left and cruise on a slight downhill grade to Kestrel Trail #39A. Turn right on Kestrel and enjoy the moderate descent down the nose of the ridge to Owls Roost Trail #37. Turn left on Owls Roost and it's 1.2 miles and a gentle downhill back to the trailhead.

The Hike: This is a very substantial foothills hike at 10.5 miles, but it's well worth it. Be sure to bring plenty of food and water. Start early in the day to avoid the heat.

The Run: This is a challenging 2+-hour run – great for Robie Creek training. Conserve energy on the climbs and enjoy the fun downhill. – Boise Bs and SS

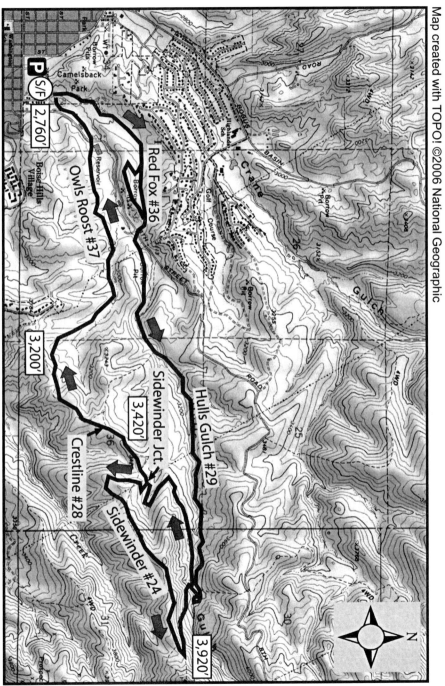

Map created with TOPO! ©2006 National Geographic

#52 Hulls Gulch Interpretive Trail

Location: Boise Central Foothills
Difficulty: Strenuous
Distance: 11.5 miles
Tread: All singletrack
Hiking time: 5 hours
Running time: 2.5 hours
Vertical gain: 2,106 feet
Watch out for: Mountain bikers in lower Hulls Gulch. The Interpretive Trail is closed to biking.
Season: April – October. Winter use may be feasible in the lower end

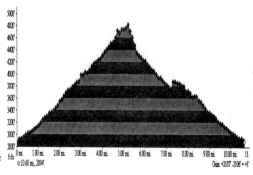

Getting there: From downtown Boise, take North 8th Street several miles through the North End until the pavement ends. Continue on 8th Street for a ¼ mile to a trailhead on the right side of the road. The hike/run starts here.

General remarks: There are several ways to approach this hike/run. If you want to go the full distance, follow the main directions. If you want to shorten the route, you have two choices: 1. Start and finish at the motorcycle parking lot 3 miles up 8th Street and drop into the Hulls Interpretive Trail from there; 2. **Shuttle**: Park a vehicle at the lower 8th Street parking area and then drive another vehicle up 8th Street to the upper Interpretive Trail parking area, and then hike/run down Hulls for about 5 miles.

Directions: Follow signs for Hulls Gulch Trail #29. It's about 2.5 miles from the trailhead to the Hulls-Crestline junction. Go straight here and follow the narrow singletrack up the creek-bottom. At mile 4.5, you'll come to a fork in the trail. Stay right to tour the headwaters and check out the waterfall. At the top of the trail, bear left to do a short loop up the hill toward the upper parking area and then loop back to the Interpretive Trail. On the way down, you can bear right at the fork leading to the 8th Street Motorcycle Parking Lot, and then drop back into Hulls Gulch for another short loop for variation. Continue to cruise down Hulls back to the trailhead.

The Hike: It's a very pleasant hike up Hulls Gulch to the headwaters and the upper Boise Foothills. There's a bonus at the top: a cool waterfall. You'll feel like you've got your own private Idaho after leaving the Hulls-Crestline intersection because few people use the Interpretive Trail. Pack plenty of food and water and enjoy yourself.

The Run: For strong runners, this is a popular and beautiful route. The gradient isn't too steep, but it's steady and strenuous at times. The trail tread is nice and firm, and sweet and narrow in the upper reach of the trail. You'll cross the creek several times on bridges. Be sure to carry water and snacks because travel time is over two hours.
 – Lynette McDougal and SS

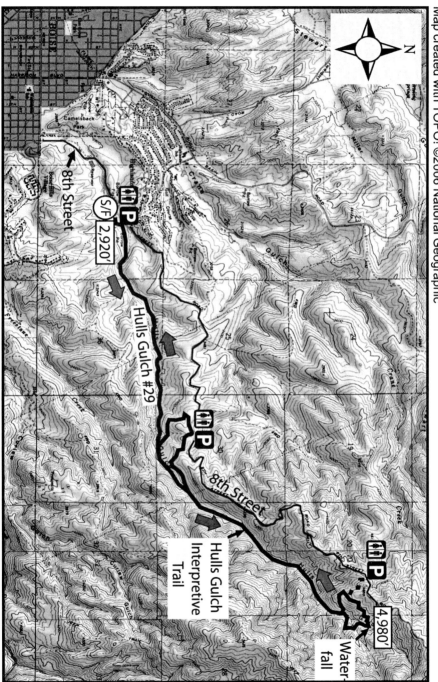

Map created with TOPO! ©2006 National Geographic

N

8th Street

S/F 2,920'

Hulls Gulch #29

8th Street

Hulls Gulch Interpretive Trail

4,980'

Water- fall

#53 Camelsback - Hulls - Bob's Loop

Location: Boise Central Foothills
Difficulty: Strenuous uphill; rock-slalom downhill
Distance: 6.4 miles
Tread: Singletrack
Hiking time: 2:45
Running time: 1:20
Vertical gain/loss: 1,077 feet/689 feet
Watch out for: Mountain bikers, dogs and other trail users

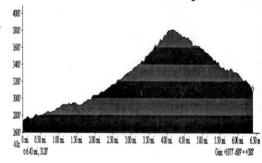

Water: Seasonal in Hulls Gulch and Crane Gulch
Season: March - October; winter use may be feasible if trails are frozen.

Getting there: From downtown Boise, take N. 13th Street to Heron Street, turn right and pull into the parking lot for Camelsback Park. The hike/run starts here. **Shuttle**: Plant a vehicle at the end of Hearthstone Drive. Take Bogus Basin Road to a stop sign at Curling Drive. Take Curling to Breamere, turn left, and follow Breamere to Hearthstone. Go left and follow the road to the dead end circle.

General notes: This is a Boise Foothills classic climber's special. It's a beautiful cruise on Red Fox and Chickadee Ridge to Hulls Gulch, and then a steady climb up Hulls and even steeper ascent to the motorcycle parking lot on 8th Street. From there, it's a slight downhill glide on Trail #1 and an all-downhill rock-slalom on Bob's.
Directions: From Camelsback, run on the grass behind the tennis courts and head east over to the trailhead. Stay to the left side of the ponds and proceed up Red Fox Trail #36. After the first hill, watch for a right-hand turn for Chickadee Ridge, Trail #36A. Turn right and scale the ridge. After the trail rejoins Red Fox, go around the gate, cross 8th Street, and bear left on Hulls Gulch Trail #29. Cross the bridge and go left at the Red Cliffs junction, and head up Hulls. It's about 2.2 miles of climbing from here to the Hulls-Crestline junction. Watch your footing – tap dance around the rocks. At the Living Room junction (Maggie's term for the social take-a-breather spot), get a sip of water and get ready for a nasty steep climb up to the motorcycle parking lot. It's only a few minutes of agony! Once at the top, you've covered 4 miles and 1,077' of ascent. Now the fun begins. Cross 8th Street, turn left and pick up Trail #1, a singletrack, on the upper shoulder of the road. Follow Trail #1 a little less than a mile to the Bob's Trail #30 junction on the left side of a hairpin turn. Drop into Bob's and let 'er rip downhill. There are many rock gardens and big-boulder obstacles on the way down.

The Hike: The Hulls-Bob's loop provides some nice variation from the norm. Lots of nice singletrack creekside hiking to enjoy.
The Run: It's a long, tough climb to the motorcycle parking lot, but after that, it's a fun cruise downhill. Enjoy! – Boise Bs and SS

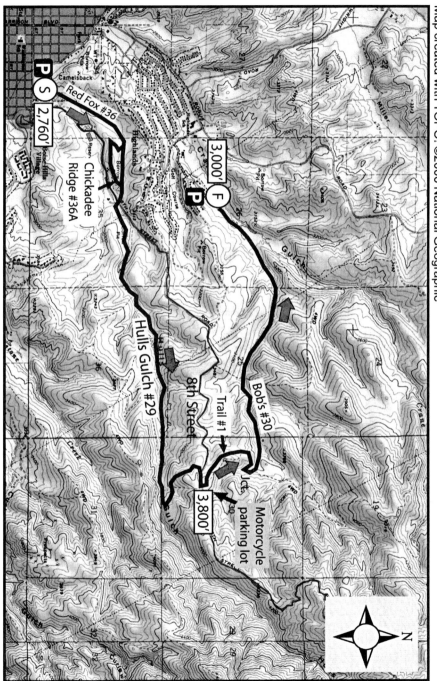

#54 Jumpin' Jeepers Figure 8 Loop

Location: Military Reserve Park
Difficulty: Strenuous, with easy to moderate sections
Distance: 6.75 miles
Tread: Dirt road, singletrack
Hiking time: 2.5-3 hours
Running time: 1:20
Vertical gain/loss: 1,000 feet
Watch out for: Mountain bikers and dogs on the loose
Water: Dependable in pond near trailhead; seasonal in Cottonwood Creek.

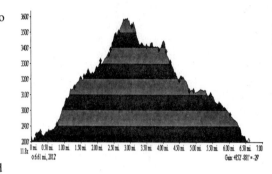

Season: March - October; winter use may be feasible when trails are frozen.

Getting there: From downtown Boise, take State Street east to Fort Street, and then turn left on Reserve Street. Go about a half mile and turn left on Mountain Cove Road. Follow that to a right-hand corner and proceed 100 yards to the Military Reserve trailhead on the right. The hike/run starts here.

General notes: If you'd like to maximize your mileage and workout in Military Reserve Park, this hike/run is for you. It features strenuous climbing to reach the Central Ridge, provides a breather until you get to Shane's Loop, and then another tough climb to the top of Shane's Summit. From there, it's a really fun and scenic cruise down Bucktail and the Central Ridge back to the trailhead. The name for this loop comes from the possibility of gunfire noise coming from the Boise Police gun range below the Bucktail Trail. I was enjoying an awesome sunset and absolute quiet in near-dark conditions, only to hear rapid gunfire that caused me to jump out of my skin.

Directions: Head up Toll Road Trail #27A, cross the creek, and continue up the trail. Turn left at the Eagle Ridge junction and climb Trail #20 to the top of the Central Ridge (mile 1.1). Turn right and follow Central Ridge Trail #22 to Shane's (mile 1.8). Bear left to do the Shane's Loop clockwise. It's a strenuous climb up the grade to Shane's Summit. You've climbed 1,000 feet over 3 miles. Take a moment to catch your breath. Keep going straight and descend to the Shane's-Rocky Canyon connector trail junction. Take a hard right on #26A and cruise on buttery smooth singletrack. The trail bends to the left and goes downhill to the Shane's-Bucktail junction (mile 4.2). Bear right on Bucktail #20A and follow that to Central Ridge Trail #22 to finish the route.

The Hike: This is a strenuous hike with many easy-going pitches as well that provides a great tour of the upper reaches of Military Reserve Park.
The Run: This is a challenging run with some steep climbs and fun singletrack cruising. To mix things up, try reversing the route the next time you do it. – SS

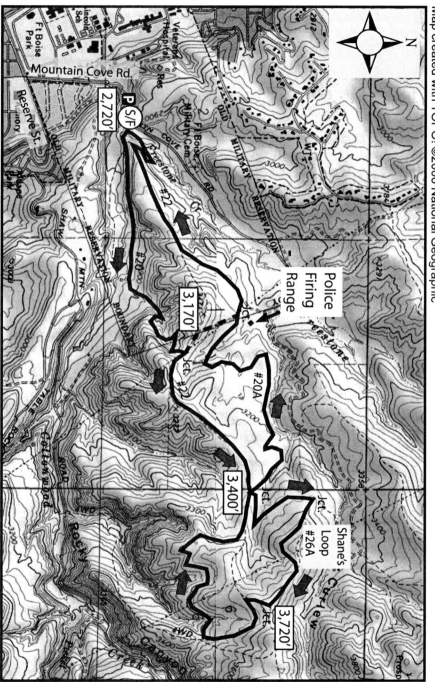

Map created with TOPO! ©2006 National Geographic

2,720'

Mountain Cove Rd.

Ft Boise Park

Lincoln Sch

Reserve St.

Police Firing Range

3,170'

3,400'

Shane's Loop #26A

3,720'

#22

#20

#20A

#22

N

#55 Military Reserve - Sidewinder Loop

Location: Military Reserve Park
Difficulty: Strenuous to moderate
Distance: 7 miles
Tread: Singletrack, dirt road
Hiking time: 2:30 hours
Running time: 1:20 minutes
Vertical gain/loss: 1,181 feet
Watch out for: Mountain bikers and other trail users
Water: Seasonal in Freestone Creek
Season: Year-round; winter use may be feasible when trails are frozen.

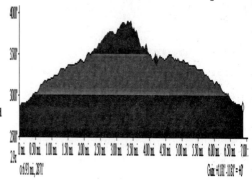

Getting there: From downtown Boise, take State Street east to Fort Street, and then turn left on Reserve Street. Go about a half mile and turn left on Mountain Cove Road. Follow it for 1 mile to a parking lot and trailhead on the right. The hike/run starts here.

General notes: This route requires a fair bit of steep climbing, especially on the Military Reserve Connector trail and second half of Sidewinder. But the route in between on the Crestline Trail has a pretty darn reasonable grade. On the way down, the views are spectacular and the descent is easy-going after the steep grade going down Trail #4. It's a great half-day hike or a fairly taxing but fun cruiser of a run.

Directions: Head north on the road to a dirt driveway on the left, where a singletrack takes off to the left of the driveway. This is the Military Reserve Connector Trail to Crestline. It's slightly less than a mile of steep climbing to Crestline, aka the Freeway. Go right on the Freeway. The gradient gets easier now. Climb to Sidewinder junction at mile 2.1. Go right and climb a mile and a half on Sidewinder to the top. Take a moment to enjoy the view. You've traved 3.5 miles and climbed over 1,000 feet to reach Sidewinder Saddle. Go left and head down Trail #4 a half mile to Crestline, turn left and retrace your steps to the trailhead. It's a delightful downhill cruise.

The Hike: This is a nice hike close to town that provides a great workout and sweet views of the valley. Bring a snack or lunch and beverages and take a break at the peak of the hike at Sidewinder - Trail #4 junction to enjoy the setting.

The Run: This is a fun and challenging running route that guarantees a good workout. To mix things up, try reversing the Trail #4 - Sidewinder loop the next time you do it. – SS

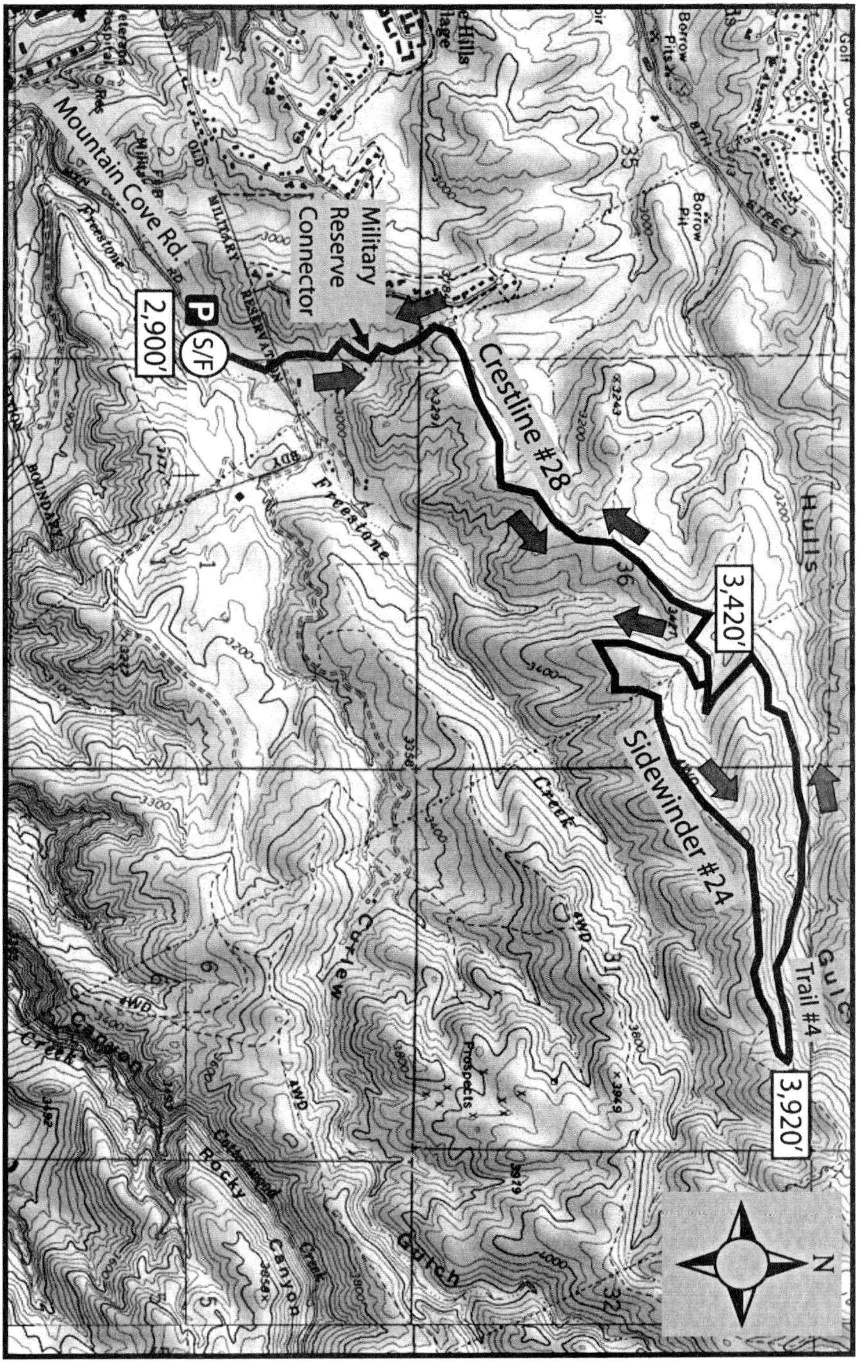

Map created with TOPO! ©2006 National Geographic

Mountain Cove Rd

Military Reserve Connector

2,900'

P S/F

Crestline #28

3,420'

Hulls

Sidewinder #24

Gulch Trail #4

3,920'

Freestone

Creek

Curlew

Creek

Prospects

Rocky Canyon

Gulch

Cottonwood Creek

N

#56 Three Bears Loop

Location: East Boise Foothills
Difficulty: Strenuous uphill; steep
downhill
Distance: 6.5 miles
Tread: Dirt road, singletrack
Hiking time: 2+ hours
Running time: 1 hour
Vertical gain/loss: 1,295 feet
Watch out for: Speeding vehicles on
Rocky Canyon Road and other trail
users

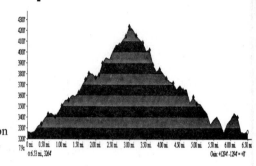

Water: Seasonal in Cottonwood Creek
Season: March - October; winter use is not normally feasible.

Getting there: From downtown Boise, take State Street east to Fort Street. Turn left
on Reserve Street. Follow Reserve to Shaw Mountain Road and take the road to the top
of the grade. Bear left on Rocky Canyon Road. Stay on the paved road to a right-hand
pull-out .5 miles after the end of the pavement. The hike/run starts here.

General notes: Three Bears is a challenging hike/run in the Rocky Canyon zone of the
Boise Foothills. It's a moderate but steady climb up Rocky Canyon Road to the Three
Bears junction, and then a heinous climb to Curlew Ridge. Then it's all downhill – and
fairly steep on the narrow ridge – back to the start. Watch for hawks and other wildlife
on the way down.

Directions: From the pullout, head up Rocky Canyon Road about 2 miles to the
junction with the Three Bears Trail. The turnoff is the first trail on the left after the
steep climb beginning at the cattle guard. Once the road levels out, watch for the hard-
left on Three Bears Trail #26, and climb the steep grade for 1.5 miles to Curlew Ridge.
Take a moment to enjoy the high point of the trail. Turn left to head down the ridge
about 3 miles to the top of Shane's. Turn left at Shane's #26A, and descend to Rocky
Canyon Road. Ignore the right-hand turn for Shane's loop on your way down.

The Hike: This is a great off-the-beaten-path hike. Enjoy it.

The Run: Try this loop in a counter-clockwise direction to increase the uphill workout
(increases rating to gonzo uphill); otherwise, lots of of fun downhill going down
Curlew Ridge. You may run into sheep grazing in the spring. Also, watch for birds of
prey flying overhead and big game, particularly in the late fall and early spring.
– Lynette McDougal and SS

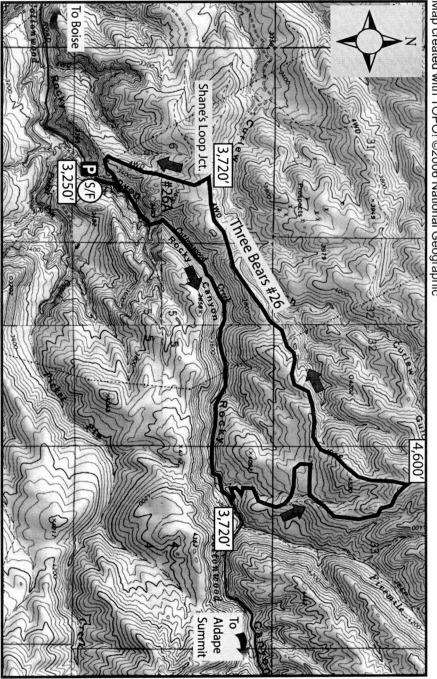

To Boise

Shane's Loop Jct.

3,720'

#26A

3,250'

P S/F

Three Bears #26

4,600'

3,720'

To Aldape Summit

#57 Foothills on the Rocks (Table Rock)

Location: Table Rock in East Boise
Difficulty: Strenuous to gonzo, with moderate pitches in between
Distance: 4.35 miles
Tread: Singletrack
Hiking time: 1.5 hours
Running time: 55 minutes
Vertical gain/loss: 952 feet
Watch out for: Mountain bikers and steep grades
Water: None unless there's potholes of water on the trail
Season: March - October; winter use may be feasible when trails are frozen.

Getting there: From the intersection of Broadway and Warm Springs Avenue in east Boise, go east on Warm Springs past the M&W market to Old Penitentiary Road. Turn left and go straight toward the Old Pen. Turn left at the end of the boulevard and follow signs for public parking by the Bishop's House. The hike/run starts here.

General notes: Foothills on the Rocks takes you on a full tour of Castle Rock and Table Rock, while dishing up a gonzo-steep climb to the top of Table Rock and great views. Tim Breuer, former Ridge to Rivers trail coordinator, named this route. Shake, do not stir. This is a double-pull route, with a short, fairly steep climb to the top of Castle Rock, a moderate cruise over to the shoulder of Table Rock, and the painful heart-pounding climb to the top of Table Rock. After that's over, you'll circumnavigate the top of Table Rock adjacent to the quarry, and return to the trailhead.
Directions: Head up Castle Rock Trail #19 and climb .5 miles to the top of the spiky basalt rock cap overlooking Quarry View Park. Turn right at the top and take the Quarry Trail along the edge of the rocks (watch your footing), pick up Trail #15 and cruise over to the west flank of Table Rock. The trail gets progressively steeper as you approach the south face of the mountain. Pace yourself. At the switchback corner, pause to check out the geological interpretive signs. Continue the last grade to the top. Go over to the cross and check out the view. There's a bench there to take a breather. Head east on the road over to the northeast edge of the plateau and pick up Trail #16, a singletrack. Follow it around the edge of the Quarry and bear right on Trail #17. Thread through giant boulders. The trail rejoins Trail #15. Retrace your steps to the Castle Rock-Table Rock junction, go left and descend on Trail #15 to the trailhead.

The Hike: This hike provides a great workout very close to town. Bring a snack and water to enjoy the views on top.

The Run: This is a grueling run that will test the best. You could call the climb to Table Rock "heart attack" hill. Don't go too hard. Once you're on top, it's a fun scenic cruise back to the trailhead. – SS

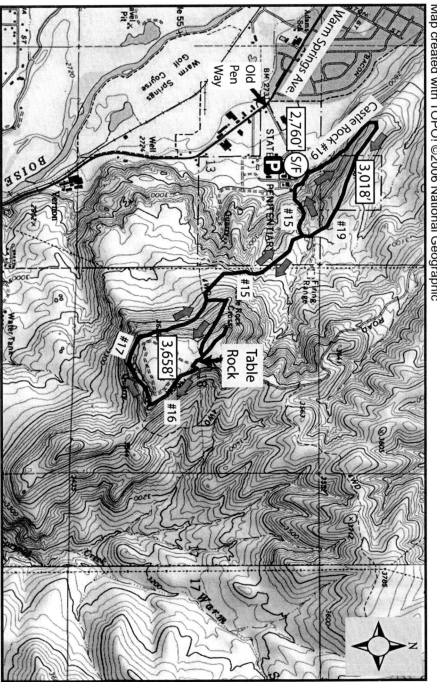

Map created with TOPO! ©2006 National Geographic

#58 Candyland Table Rock Loop

Location: East Boise Foothills
Difficulty: Moderate to gonzo
Distance: 6 miles
Tread: Paved path, singletrack
Hiking time: 2:30+
Running time: 1:20
Vertical gain/loss: 1,136'
Watch out for: Wildlife and other trail users
Water: Dry except for rain water in potholes
Season: March - October; winter use may be feasible when trails are frozen

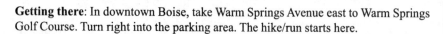

Getting there: In downtown Boise, take Warm Springs Avenue east to Warm Springs Golf Course. Turn right into the parking area. The hike/run starts here.

General notes: Candyland, a name created by the Boise Bs, features a great tour of Castle Rock, Table Rock, the new Rock Island trail and the new trail that connects to Warm Springs Golf Course. You warm up on the Greenbelt, climb Castle Rock, and the south face of Table Rock, and then the fun begins. It's a cool downhill to take Trail #16 around the basalt cap rocks, and Trail #17 by the quarry, and then you descend on new twisting and winding trails to Warm Springs Golf Course. At the end of the run, one of the Bs said, "That's just like Candyland," referring to the rainbow-colored kids' board game. Be sure to bring a snack and water.

Directions: Pick up the Greenbelt next to the golf pro shop, and head west about a mile to a right-hand neighborhood cutoff trail that leaves the main Greenbelt. It brings you to Warm Springs Avenue. Cross the road with caution (busy street) and take Old Penitentiary Road to a main junction one-half mile ahead. Turn left and follow signs for a public parking area and trailhead. Turn left on Trail #19 and climb a steady grade to the top of Castle Rock. Bear left on #19 and cruise over a rock ledge over to Table Rock Trail #15. Follow #15 to the top of Table Rock; it gets progressively steeper toward the top. Go touch the cross for good luck, and then follow the dirt road toward the foothills (north) over to Trail #16. It wraps around the top of the rock, and links to Trail #17 next to the Quarry. Continue descending on #17 until you see a left-hand turn for Trail #16. Go left and and then right on Rock Island Trail #16B and follow the switchbacks and rock features down to Trail #14, the Tram Trail. Turn right and descend on #14 to the golf course parking lot.

The Hike: This is a challenging hike featuring a full tour of Castle Rock, Table Rock and the cool new trails that connect to the golf couse. Bring plenty of food and water.
The Run: This route packs a major punch. It's a great workout, grinding up the south face of Table Rock. And you'll enjoy the twisting features on the way down. – SS

#59 - #60 Squaw Creek Loops

Location: Boise River Wildlife
Management Area
Difficulty: Strenuous to gonzo
Distance: Long loop: 7.9 miles;
short loop: 6.25 miles
Tread: Dirt two-track and
singletrack
Hiking time: Long loop: 3 hours;
short loop: 2:30
Running time: Long loop: 1:50;
short loop: 1:25

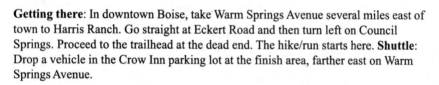

Vertical gain: 1,633 feet long loop; 1,327 feet short loop.
Watch out for: Wildlife and wildflowers
Water: Dry except for rain water potholes
Season: April 15 – October; Area is closed during the winter as a big game preserve.

Getting there: In downtown Boise, take Warm Springs Avenue several miles east of
town to Harris Ranch. Go straight at Eckert Road and then turn left on Council
Springs. Proceed to the trailhead at the dead end. The hike/run starts here. **Shuttle**:
Drop a vehicle in the Crow Inn parking lot at the finish area, farther east on Warm
Springs Avenue.

General notes: The Squaw Creek loops are steep and challenging, but the surrounding
countryside is a beautiful place to experience, particularly in the spring when
wildflowers are blooming and everything is deep green. Note that the Boise River
Wildlife Management Area is dedicated to protecting wintering deer and elk herds, so
it is closed to public use between Dec. 1 and April 15. Runners and hikers should try
the short loop first, and then try the longer route if you're up to it.

Directions: Head up Squaw Creek Trail #12. It climbs at a steep clip right off the bat
for less than a mile. It levels off and climbs again over several heinous pitches to an
initial summit at mile 2.2. Now the trail descends and bobs up and down over to
another heinous climb to the junction with Trail #13, the Cobb Trail at mile 3.5. Bail
off to the right to do the short loop. Otherwise, keep climbing up the next and last
gonzo steep pitch (lots of loose rock) to the next saddle, and take a breather. It's pretty
much on the level or downhill from here. You'll contour to the east, past the junction
with Trail E, and peel off to the right on Trail #11, a singletrack at mile 5.5. Now it's a
fun, ripping descent to the trailhead and Crow Inn.

The Hike: As temperatures warm up, this hike is best done in the morning or evening.
The Run: It's a mondo trail-running experience to conquer Squaw Creek trail. It's
going to hurt, and that's part of the charm. Do the short loop first, and you should be
good to go on the longer route next time. – SS

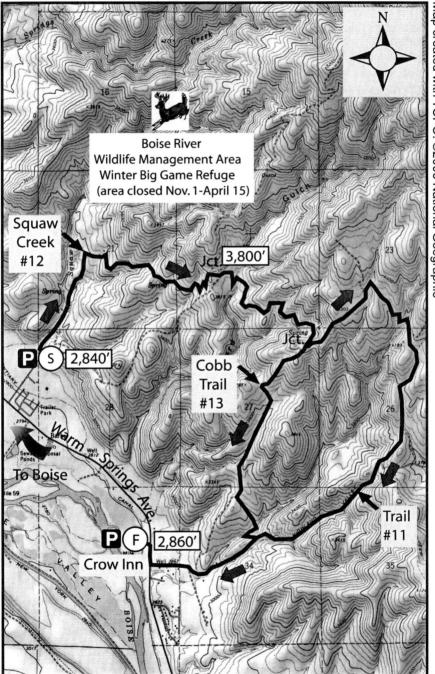

Boise River
Wildlife Management Area
Winter Big Game Refuge
(area closed Nov. 1–April 15)

Squaw
Creek
#12

Jct. 3,800'

P S 2,840'

Cobb
Trail
#13

To Boise

P F 2,860'

Crow Inn

Trail
#11

N

Map created with TOPO! ©2006 National Geographic

#61 Twin Peaks at Bogus Basin Loop

Location: Bogus Basin Ski Resort
Difficulty: Strenuous to gonzo
Distance: 9 miles
Tread: Singletrack, dirt road, sandy in places
Hiking time: 4 hours
Running time: 2 hours
Vertical gain: 2,509 feet
Watch out for: Wildlife, wildflowers, other trail users
Water: Yes, at the Shafer Butte picnic area or mountain springs
Season: June - October

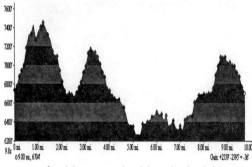

Getting there: From downtown Boise, take Harrison Boulevard north to the intersection of Bogus Basin Road and Hill Road. Go straight (north) on Bogus Basin road for approximately 18 miles to the lower lodge. Keep going on the road. Pavement gives way to dirt for a short time, and then you'll see a right-turn for the Pioneer Lodge. Follow the paved road to the lodge. The hike/run starts here.

General notes: This is a triple-pull hike/run that guarantees a great workout. You'll climb to the top of Shafer Butte, and then tour around Mores Mountain before climbing back to Bogus to finish the route. When the weather gets hot in the Boise Valley in July, it's a perfect time to head up to Bogus where the temperatures can be 10-20 degrees cooler. Be sure to pack plenty of water and food for this one. You'll need it.

Directions: Head out of the Pioneer Lodge parking lot, climb to the top of Morning Star chairlift, and turn left on Lodge Trail #140. Follow that for a quarter-mile or so to Tempest Trail #95 on the right. Here's a gonzo climb up a series of switchbacks to the top of Superior Chairlift #3. Descend on the dirt road switchbacks over to the Majestic ski slope and turn left to follow the dirt road heading downhill to the saddle to the Shafer Butte picnic area. (Don't miss this turn or you'll end up on the Paradise side of the mountain; see map). At the picnic area, fill up on water, as needed. At the north end of the picnic area, pick up the Mores Mountain Trail, a downhill singletrack that winds along the east side of Mores Mountain. You'll pop out on the Boise Ridge Road #190. Turn left. In a mile, you'll see a signed turnoff for the Shafer Butte picnic area. Go left and climb back to the picnic area (steep) and then climb back to Bogus via the Majestic dirt road. The road climbs to Lodge Trail #140 (may not be marked). At a fork junction, ignore the switchback climbing to the top of Shafer Butte and go straight on Lodge Trail. Now it's an easy cruise back to the Pioneer Lodge.

The Hike/Run: Don't let the mileage fool you – this is a stout hike/run with 2,500 feet of climbing. Carry plenty of water and snacks, and pace yourself. Watch out for weird footing on slick granite roads and trails. – Lynette McDougal and SS

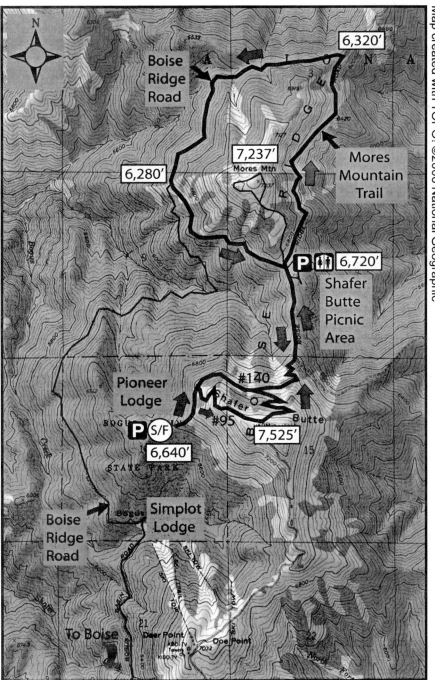

Boise Ridge Road

6,320'

Mores Mountain Trail

7,237'
Mores Mtn

6,280'

P 🚻 6,720'
Shafer Butte Picnic Area

Pioneer Lodge

#140

Shafer

#95

Butte

P S/F
6,640'

7,525'

Boise Ridge Road

Simplot Lodge

To Boise

Deer Point

Doe Point

#62 Cottonwood Creek out and back

Location: Boise National Forest, near Arrowrock Reservoir
Difficulty: Strenuous to gonzo
Distance: 18 miles
Tread: Singletrack
Hiking time: 6-8 hours
Running time: 3+ hours
Vertical gain: 3,873 feet
Watch out for: Wildlife, stream crossings
Water: Dependable in Cottonwood Creek
Season: May - October

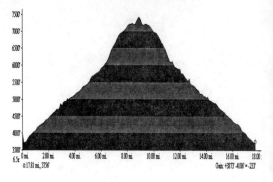

Getting there: From downtown Boise, take Warm Springs Avenue east to Idaho 21. Turn left on Idaho 21 and follow it 16 miles to the Mores Creek high bridge and turn right on USFS Road #268, the road to Spring Shores marina. Drive 15 miles along Lucky Peak and Arrowrock to a junction with USFS Road #377. Turn left and follow #377 3 miles to the Cottonwood Creek Trailhead on the right. The hike/run starts here.

General notes: This is a sweet forest hike close to Boise. The best approach is to head up the trail 3 to 5 miles, have lunch in the shade of a ponderosa pine, and go back. I'm including the whole 18-mile enchilada for hard-core types. Power-hikers training for a big event and strong and experienced trail runners will enjoy the challenge. Be sure to pack plenty of food and drink and bring the wildflower guide.

Directions: Head up Cottonwood Creek Trail #189. It starts out a steep grade, and remains at a continuously uphill clip for the whole duration. There will be numerous stream crossings on the way up the Cottonwood Creek Trail – more than 20 in all. Several wildfires have burned through the creek-bottom; watch for signs. More than 7 miles up the trail, you'll encounter several bogs and small creek crossings. You're getting close to the ridgetop! At mile 8.4, the trail pops out on the dirt road heading to Thorn Butte Lookout. Mark your location. The trailhead sign may not be in place. You've climbed 3,320 vertical feet. Ponder the optional 500-foot .6-mile climb to the top of the Lookout on the road, or turn around and head back down the trail.

The Hike: You make the call on how far you want to go. There are many ponderosa pines to hide under for shade or a nap.

The Run: If the hike is grueling, the 18-mile run is totally gonzo to scale the creekside trail to Thorn Butte Lookout and go back. Only strong long-distance runners should attempt it. Others should run as far as you like. Dance over the rocks to keep your feet dry. – SS

Map created with TOPO! ©2006 National Geographic

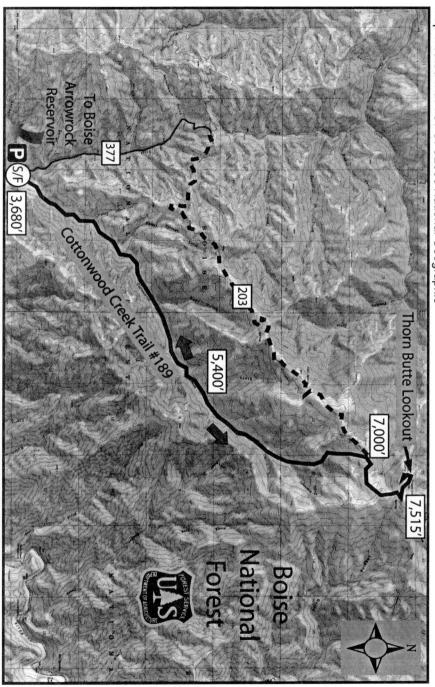

To Boise
Arrowrock
Reservoir

377

P S/F 3,680'

Cottonwood Creek Trail #189

203

5,400'

Thorn Butte Lookout

7,000'

7,515'

Boise National Forest

FOREST SERVICE
U S
DEPARTMENT OF AGRICULTURE

N

#63 Pilot Peak out and back

Location: Mores Creek Summit, Boise
National Forest, NE of Idaho City
Difficulty: Strenuous
Distance: 7.9 miles
Tread: 4WD dirt road
Hiking time: 3:30
Running time: 1:20
Vertical loss/gain: 2,043 feet
Watch out for: Motor vehicles, ATVs,
other trail users
Water: Possible isolated water holes or
springs
Season: June-November

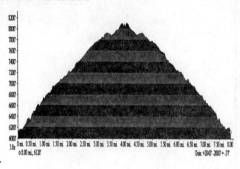

Getting there: From Boise, take Idaho 21 east to Idaho City. Continue east on ID 21 approximately 13 miles to Mores Creek Summit. There is a large parking area and rest room on the right side of the road. Park. The hike/run starts here.

General notes: Pilot Peak is steeper and more direct (1.5 miles shorter) than the round-trip to Sunset Mountain Lookout (9.4 miles). It's a pretty continuous uphill grade on the Pilot Peak Road (USFS 380). The road gets away from the highway pretty quick, and there are great views of Freeman Peak across the draw. Take a lunch and plenty of water and enjoy your time at the summit. Bring a wildflower guide – there are flowers galore up there in June and July.

Directions: Head out of the Mores Creek parking lot, cross Idaho 21, and head up the Pilot Peak Road (USFS 380). This is the main route to the top. No significant junctions exist in the first three miles. At mile 3.2, you'll reach a three-way junction at a saddle. Take a hard right and cruise up to the summit of Pilot Peak. The road isn't as steep in this section. It's slightly over a .5 miles to the top. Enjoy the views of the Boise National Forest, and the Sawtooths in the distance. You've climbed 2,043 vertical feet over 3.9 miles. Retrace your steps to return to the trailhead.

The Hike: Adventuresome hikers may want to try taking the ridgeline back down the mountain from the top of Pilot Peak. Just make sure you take the *right* ridge (the one directly above the road), and then drop down to the Pilot Peak road in the last mile. It gets very brushy toward the bottom. In the winter, many of us backcountry ski up that ridge to some great powder slopes.

The Run: It's a steep climb to the top of Pilot Peak, so conserve energy and take it easy. The grade remains constant most of the way to the saddle at mile 3.2. From that point onward, the climbing is more moderate, and then all downhill on the way back. Be sure to carry some water and a snack for a short rest at the summit. – SS

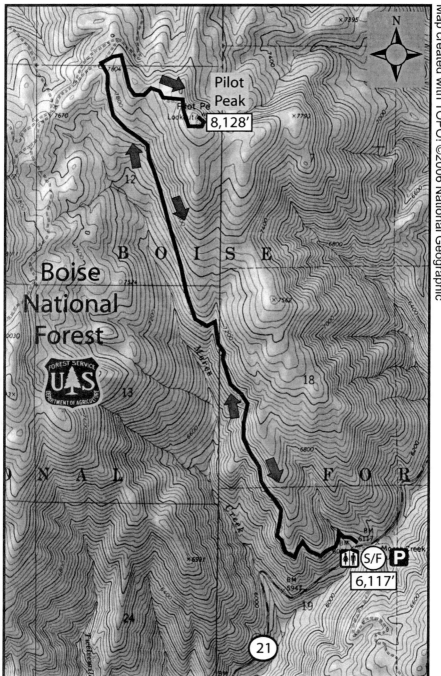

Map created with TOPO! ©2006 National Geographic

Pilot Peak
8,128'

Boise National Forest

BOISE

Boise
National
Forest

FOR

6,117'

21

157

#64 Sunset Lookout out and back

Location: Mores Creek Summit,
northeast of Idaho City
Difficulty: Strenuous
Distance: 9.4 miles
Tread: 4WD dirt road
Hiking time: 4-5 hours
Running time: 2:30
Vertical loss/gain: 1,800 feet
Watch out for: Motor vehicles, ATVs,
other trail users
Water: Isolated springs
Season: June - October

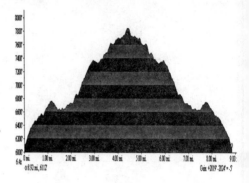

Getting there: From Boise, take Idaho 21 east to Idaho City. Continue east on Idaho 21 approximately 13 miles to Mores Creek Summit. There is a large parking area and rest room on the right side of the road. Park. The hike/run starts here.

General notes: This is a cool hike/run even though it's on a 4WD dirt road, because it leads to a forest lookout that provides awesome views of the mountains in the Boise National Forest. Also, the road does not get that much traffic. Be sure to pack plenty of water, a lunch and snacks to enjoy your time at the top of Sunset Mountain. The fire lookout is typically manned in the summer months, so please observe their privacy. Bring a wildflower guide.

Directions: Head out of the parking lot and climb up USFS Road #316. This is your main route to the top. The road climbs at a steep gradient in the first mile, but it mellows after a bit and never gets any steeper than that. At 1.2 miles, you get a peek at the lookout above. Ignore right-hand spur roads as you continue to climb. At 2.4 miles, the road rises at a gnarly pitch for about .5 miles and comes to a small saddle. From here, it's a steady uphill grade to the top. Take your time and pace yourself. Once on top, check out the 360-degree views. On a clear day, you can see Pilot Peak to the north, the North Fork of the Boise River to the east, and the Banner Ridge area, maybe even the Sawtooths.

The Hike: Take your time on the hike to Sunset Mountain Lookout. Conserve energy on the steep pitches. It's 4.7 miles to the top and just shy of 1,800 feet of vertical gain. Yield to motor vehicles and ATVs coming up and down the trail.

The Run: It's a steep climb to the top of Sunset Mountain, so take it easy. But there also are sections where the steepness abates and the climbing is more moderate. Be sure to carry some water and a snack for a short rest at the summit. – SS

Map created with TOPO! ©2006 National Geographic

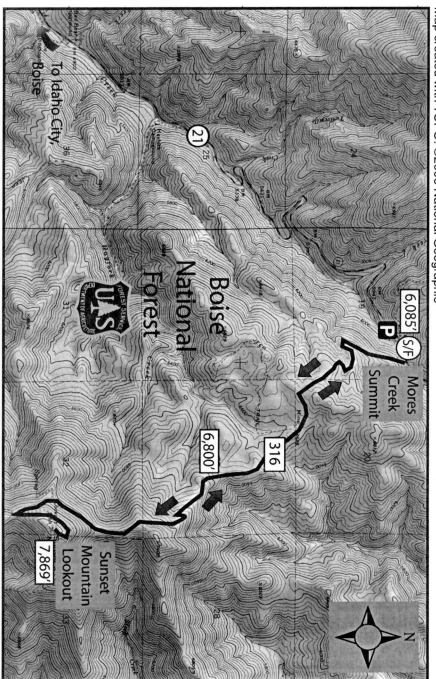

To Idaho City,
Boise

21

Boise
National
Forest

6,085' S/F

P

Mores
Creek
Summit

6,800'

316

Sunset
Mountain
Lookout

7,869'

N

159

#65 Zimmer Creek Loop

Location: Near Banks, Idaho
Difficulty: Strenuous
Distance: 9 miles
Tread: Two-track, singletrack
Hiking time: 4 hours
Running time: 2 hours or less
Vertical gain: 2,235 feet
Watch out for: Interesting animal tracks:
deer, elk, coyote
Water: Dependable along Zimmer
Creek; many other springs
Season: Late April-October

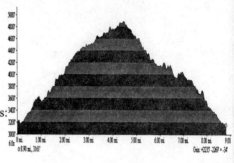

Getting there: Take Idaho 55 North to Banks. Keep going straight through Banks, as if you're heading for McCall, for another 3 miles to a roadside pull-out on the right before the railroad bridge. The hike/run starts here.

General notes: This is a great off-the-beaten-path hike/run in an open forest setting. The trail climbs high above the North Fork of the Payette River, and passes through many aspen stands, so it is beautiful scenery much of the way. Lots of wild game hang out in this area, so you are likely to see critters. Be sure to keep your dog in control. The trail climbs at a pretty reasonable grade all the way, but you climb more than 2,000 feet over 4.5 miles, so that's why this route falls into the strenuous category.

Directions: Take off from the parking area and follow the ATV trail across the creek and continue on the trail for .5 miles to a hairpin junction by the creek. Go straight here for .2 miles of a mile, and then go left on the grassy two-track trail and follow it as it contours up the mountain for the next 2.5 miles. The trail is semi-faint in places, but the old road grade is clearly visible the whole way. At mile 3, you'll pass by a knoll at 4,500 feet elevation. Now the switchbacks are over and you'll hike a "long" 2 miles out north, climbing another 600 feet on the two-track. The trail will bend sharply toward the east at least two times to pass by creeks, and then finally, the trail joins the main Zimmer Creek Trail. Turn left and follow the Zimmer Creek two-track downhill (much more heavily used) back to the start.

The Hike: This is a beautiful, but challenging hike because of the distance and elevation gain. You may feel a bit lost as you're climbing the grassy two-track on a series of spiral staircase switchbacks, but stay with the old road grade and you'll be fine. Be sure to bring a lunch and plenty of water.

The Run: It's a tough run on the Zimmer Creek Loop because of the elevation gain and distance, but it's a beautiful setting with lots of shade. Watch your footing on the grassy two-track. – SS

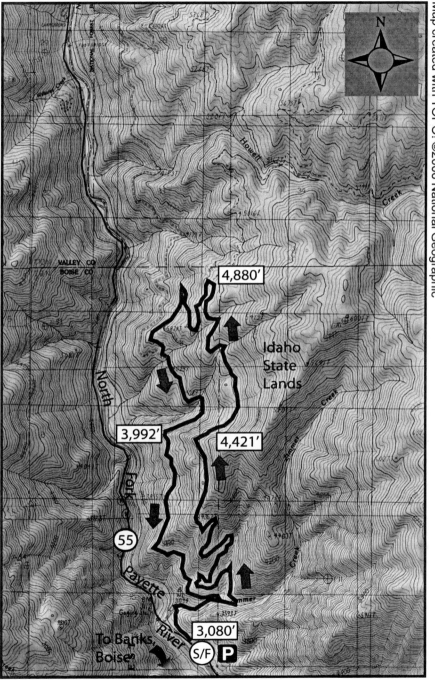

Boise Trail Guide

#66 Tripod Peak out and back

Location: Smith's Ferry
Difficulty: Strenuous
Distance: 11.8 miles out and back
Tread: All singletrack
Hiking time: 5 hours
Running time: 3 hours
Vertical gain/loss: 3,160 feet
Watch out for: Wildlife,
wildflowers and other trail users
Water: Isolated mountain springs
Season: June - October

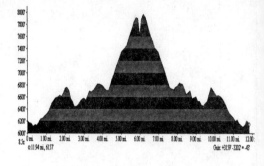

Getting there: Take Idaho 55 north about 65 miles to Smith's Ferry. Turn left by the Cougar Mountain Lodge on Forest Road #626 to Sagehen Reservoir. Follow the road about 3 miles from the highway to a signed trailhead on the right for West Mountain Trail. The hike/run starts here.

General notes: It's a beautiful mountain hike/run to Tripod Peak. It's a major climb of over 3,000 vertical feet, but the trail winds through a pine-scented forest, with great views of the surrounding countryside. Plus, it's nice to be in a shady cool forest environment a long ways from civilization. Enjoy the views of Long Valley and the Payette River to the east, Sage Hen Reservoir to the south, West Mountain, and maybe the Wallowas in Oregon and the Seven Devils to the Northwest. Be sure to bring a lunch and beverages for the summit.

Directions: Head north on West Mountain Trail #131. The trail winds through the forest and climbs to the ridge approaching Tripod Peak. The first 3 miles are reasonable, and then in the last 1.5 miles, the trail gets gonzo steep and beelines to the top of Tripod Peak over a few switchbacks. After the trail tops the ridge, turn right and head for Tripod Lookout. You've climbed 2,100 vertical feet over about 6 miles. Retrace your steps to return to the trailhead.

The Hike: This is a beautiful forest hike to an 8,000-foot peak that lords over the southern end of the West Mountains chain and Long Valley. Enjoy the hike, and be sure to bring a lunch and plenty of water. If you've got time, climb on the backbone of West Mountain to the north and check out the countryside. You're on top of the world.

The Run: This is a sweet forest run until you hit the switchbacks and the heinous steep route to the ridge top. Take your time in this section. Be sure to bring plenty of snacks and water. – SS

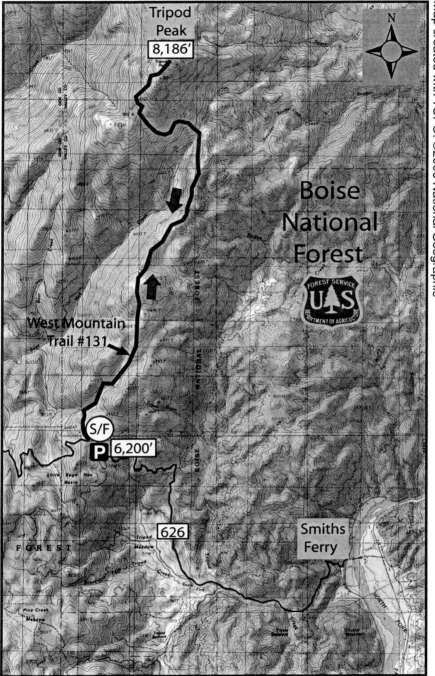

Map created with TOPO! ©2006 National Geographic

#67 One Spoon Steepness

Location: Boise National Forest, near
Crouch and Garden Valley
Difficulty: Strenuous
Distance: 5.8 miles
Tread: Singletrack
Hiking time: 2:40
Running time: NA
Vertical loss/gain: 2,633 feet
Watch out for: Wildlife
Water: Isolated springs
Season: May - November

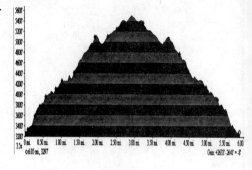

Getting there: From Boise, take Idaho 55 north to Banks (about 35 miles). Turn right after you cross the South Fork of the Payette River bridge and follow the Banks to Lowman road to the signed turnoff for Crouch. Go left, pass by the rustic little town (good coffee and food!), and follow the Middle Fork road for about 10 miles, past Tie Creek Campground, to USFS Road 698L3, a forest road on the left that crosses the Middle Fork of the Payette River. Go slow so you don't miss it. Turn left on the road, follow it for a short ways and turn left at the first fork to climb a 4WD road to a little saddle, where the marked trailhead for the One Spoon Trail #043 is located on the right. The hike/run starts here.

General notes: The One Spoon Trail is a little-known singletrack hiking trail within an hour's drive from Boise, and very close to Crouch and Garden Valley. The climb up One Spoon is very steep – it switchbacks once in a while, but generally, it just marches right up the nose of a pine-needle-covered ridge with giant ponderosa pines all around you. That's why I don't recommend the trail for running. It's just too dang steep. Great views await you on top of the Middle Fork range, a lower-slung range than most in the Payette River drainage. Bring a lunch and plenty of water and enjoy the views on top. There are several hot springs in the vicinity if you wish to take a dip after the hike.

Directions: Head up the One Spoon Trail. There are no significant trail junctions along the way except for many deer and elk trails that could cause confusion. The main thing is to stay on the ridge and keep climbing. The pine needles are so thick in places, it's almost possible to lose the trail, but if you stay on the ridge, you'll stay with the trail.

The Hike: Conserve energy and take your time as you scale the ridge. Bring a pair of binoculars to enjoy the views on top. – SS

Map created with TOPO! ©2006 National Geographic

N

Bear
Wallow
Trail

5,600'

One Spoon Trail #043

BOISE

Boom

698

To Crouch

3,400'
S/F
P

698L3

Boise
National
Forest

FOREST SERVICE
U S
DEPARTMENT OF AGRICULTURE

To Boiling
Springs

Horseshoe
Campground

#68 Snake River Petroglyph Tour

Location: Swan Falls Dam, Snake
River canyon south of Boise
Difficulty: Strenuous
Distance: 12.2 miles
Tread: Two-track, singletrack
Hiking time: 5 hours
Running time: 2+ hours
Vertical gain: 796 feet
Watch out for: Snakes in hot weather
Water: Dependable along the Snake
River
Season: Year-round, snow permitting

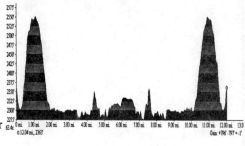

Getting there: Take I-84 west to the Kuna-Meridian exit. Turn left and follow signs to Kuna. As you pull into Kuna, you'll see signs for the Snake River Birds of Prey National Conservation Area. Turn left on the Swan Falls Road and follow to Swan Falls Dam. Park. The hike/run starts here.

General notes: This is a great tour along the Snake River canyon, with looming cliffs chock full of nesting birds of prey, primarily golden eagles, prairie falcons and hawks. The best time to do this hike/run is in the fall, winter and spring. The middle of the summer is often just too hot. Bring a lunch and plenty of water and enjoy your trip.

Directions: Take off from the parking area, cross the dam, and pick up a singletrack trail to the left, heading upstream. Turn right at the first fork and follow the two-track uphill for a short bit. At mile .9, turn right on a two-track, and then at mile 1.1, turn right again to follow a two-track that heads down along the Snake River. This is your main trail down to Wees Bar. At mile 3.2, you'll enter an old ranch. At mile 4.5, the trail bends to the left to climb around a small butte. Then you'll come to a narrow slot in a gate: pass through it and continue heading west. At mile 6, the trail braids and many boulders appear before you. Look for Indian petroglyphs. Take a break, eat your lunch, and then retrace your steps to the trailhead.

The Hike: This is a pretty easy hike because it's mostly flat, but at 12.2 miles, it's still plenty long. Take your time and enjoy it. Bring your binoculars to watch for raptors, especially in the spring.

The Run: This is a great route for a run because the trail is non-motorized on the south side of the river. It's a fun cruise along the Snake River. Bring some water and snack bars for a break at Wees Bar. – SS

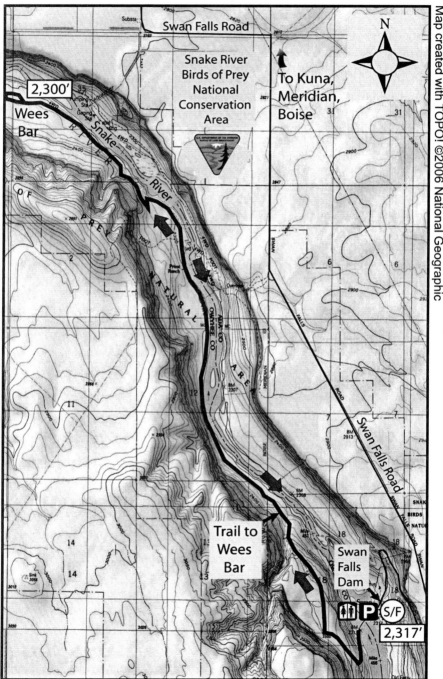

Swan Falls Road

Snake River
Birds of Prey
National
Conservation
Area

To Kuna,
Meridian,
Boise

N

2,300'

Wees
Bar

Snake River

Swan Falls Road

Trail to
Wees
Bar

Swan
Falls
Dam

S/F

2,317'

167

Epic Mountain Trails

69. Boise Ridge Climber's Special (p. 170)
70. Stueby's Death March (p. 172)
71. Race to Robie Creek course (p. 174)
72. Rocky Canyon - Trail #4 Loop (p. 176)
73. Squaw Creek Trail #8 - Trail E Loop (p. 178)
74. Thorn Butte - Cottonwood Creek Loop (p. 180)
75. Wilson Creek - Mini-Moab Loop (p. 182)

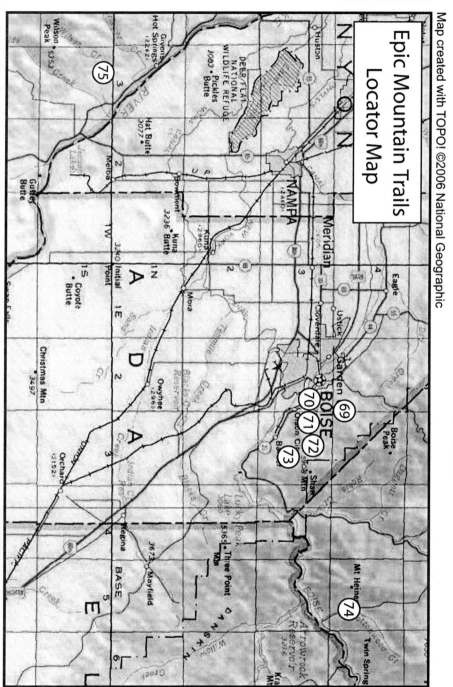

Epic Mountain Trails
Locator Map

Map created with TOPO! ©2006 National Geographic

#69 Boise Ridge Climber's Special

Location: Boise Central Foothills
Difficulty: Epic
Distance: 17.5-21.5 miles
Tread: Singletrack, dirt road
Hiking time: 7 hours
Running time: 3+ hours
Vertical gain/loss: 3,902 feet/3,635 feet
Watch out for: Mountain bikers and
other trail users
Water: Lower Hulls and Crane Creek
Season: May-October

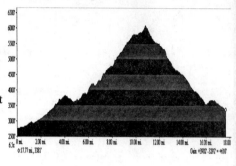

Getting there: From downtown Boise, take North 9th Street to a dead end parking area on the east edge of Camelsback Park. The hike/run starts here. **Shuttle**: Park a vehicle at the Corrals Trailhead to shave four miles off the route.

General notes: This is an epic climb, starting from Camelsback Park, with nearly 4,000 feet of vertical gain, and then a huge downhill from the top of the Boise Ridge at Eagleson Summit, elevation 6,049 feet, back to Bogus Basin Road or Camelsback. The shuttle is 17.5 miles, and the full loop is 21.5 miles. Few people would hike or run this route on purpose unless they're training for a marathon. But it is the full-on tour of the Boise Foothills for the ambitious athlete. Once you've done it, you'll do it again.

Directions: Head up Red Fox Trail #36 and follow it to 8th Street. Cross the road and bear left on Hulls #29. Climb Hulls to the junction with Crestline, and continue uphill to the motorcycle parking lot (mile 4). Cross 8th Street, and pick up Trail #1, a singletrack, on the other side of the road. Follow Trail #1 around the corner, ignore the cutoff for Bob's Trail and climb to the top of Corrals (mile 6.5). Go straight on Scott's #32 and grind it out for a mile to 8th Street. Now the steepest part is yet to come. Grunt out the steeps on upper 8th Street 2 miles to the Boise Ridge Road junction (mile 9.5). Turn left and bear left at the next junction. Follow the ridge road (not as steep) to the top of Eagleson Summit (mile 11). Take a breather! Now it's all downhill, baby. Go straight on the ridge road and descend 1 mile (watch out for deep ruts) to the Hard Guy Trail #33 on the left. Plunge down Hard Guy 5 miles. You'll go through a gate and cross a creek near the bottom before climbing again to Corrals Trail. Go right on Corrals and cruise on a slightly downhill grade to Bogus Basin Road (mile 17.5). It's another 4 miles back to Camelsback Park.

The Hike: This is a hefty hike for a day trip. Bring plenty of food and water. Start early in the day in the mid-summer to avoid the worst heat of the day.
The Run: This is a hugely challenging run. Only the most ambitious runners who like to climb for more than a half-marathon, or 20-plus miles, will enjoy this loop. Be sure to pack plenty of water and snacks. – SS

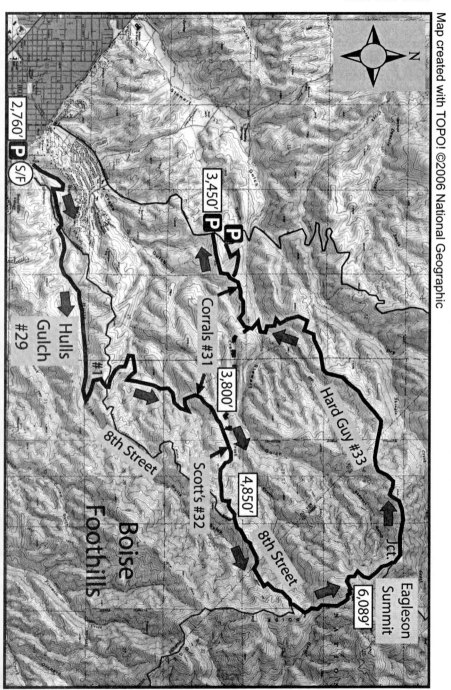

Map created with TOPO! ©2006 National Geographic

N

2,760' P P S/F

3,450' P P

Hulls Gulch #29

#1

Corrals #31

3,800'

8th Street

Scott's #32

4,850'

Hard Guy #33

Boise Foothills

8th Street

Jct.

Eagleson Summit

6,089'

#70 Stueby's Death March

Location: Boise Foothills
Difficulty: Gonzo to strenuous
Distance: 15.9
Tread: Singletrack, dirt road
Hiking time: 6 hours
Running time: 3:20
Vertical gain/loss: 1,900 feet
Watch out for: Mountain bikers, motorcycles and steep grades
Water: Seasonal in Cottonwood Creek and Freestone Creek; mostly dry ridgetop route
Season: April - October

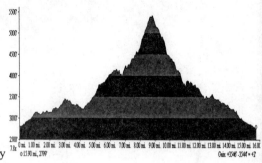

Getting there: From downtown Boise, take State Street east to Fort Street, and then turn left on Reserve Street. Go straight on Reserve and then turn left on Mountain Cove Road. Proceed on Mountain Cove past a sharp right-hand bend. Watch for the trailhead and parking area on your right. The hike/run starts here.

General notes: This is an extremely challenging route for runners and long-distance hikers. My friends named this one after I took them repeatedly on punishing mountain bike rides on this route. It's guaranteed to hurt, and hurt bad because it's got lots of steep climbing (1,900 feet of gain!). Conserve energy. Watch your footing going down Trail #4, also known as "Devil's Slide," a motorcycle trail with deep sand.

Directions: Head up Toll Road Trail #27A, cross the creek, and turn left to climb Central Ridge Trail #22. At the top, go left on #20 over to Bucktail Trail #20A. Cruise up Bucktail to Shane's Junction. Go left to the #26/#26A junction. Go left on #26 and drop into the creek, and then bear left on the dirt road downhill to the Trail #5 junction. Turn right and climb Trail #5. Look ahead and you'll see a nasty climb ahead. Take your time – there's more to come. Keep climbing until you intersect with Trail #6 at mile 6.2. Bear left and scale Trail #6 for one more nasty uphill grade to the Trail #4 junction. You made it! Turn left on Trail #4 and descend the sandy dished-out trail several miles to Sidewinder Junction at Mile 10.5. Go left on Sidewinder and follow it back to Crestline. Turn left and take Crestline back to Military Reserve Connector #23. Go left, descend to Military Reserve. Cross the dirt road and follow Freestone Trail to the trailhead.

The Hike: This is not recommended as a "fun" hike. People training for long-distance endurance hiking would benefit from doing it. Bring lots of water and snacks.
The Run: Only super-strong runners will enjoy this route. Otherwise, it will make you miserable. To mix things up, next time, try doing the loop clockwise. Climbing Trail #4 is nasty, too. – Lynette McDonald and SS

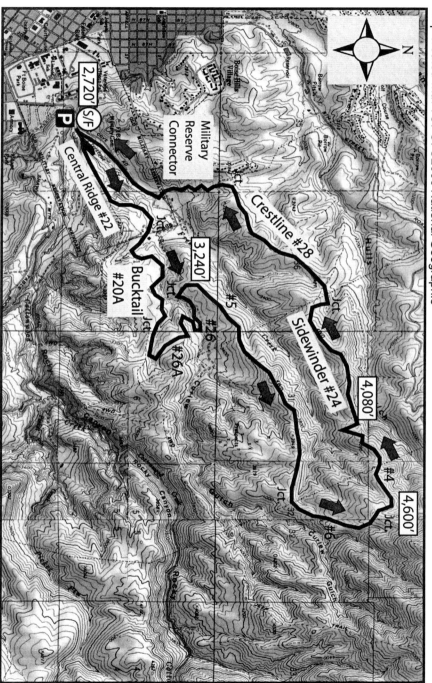

Map created with TOPO! ©2006 National Geographic

#71 Race to Robie Creek course

Location: East Boise Foothills
Difficulty: Epic
Distance: 13 miles
Tread: Paved road, dirt road
Hiking time: 4+ hours
Running time: 1:40 minutes and up
Vertical gain/loss: 2,169' gain/1,777' loss
Watch out for: Deep ruts, rocks and sand
Water: Seasonal along Cottonwood Creek
and Robie Creek.
Season: April - October

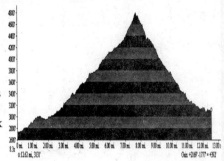

Getting there: From downtown Boise, take State Street east to Fort Street, and then turn left on Reserve Street by the Fort Boise ballfields. Go about a half mile and turn left on Mountain Cove Road and pull into the public parking area on the left. Park. The hike/run starts here.

General notes: The Race to Robie Creek has a deserved reputation as one of the most challenging half-marathons in the Northwest. It's an awesome community event, put on by runners and walkers for runners and walkers, so it's always fun. It's great to do the walk if you don't run, and if you have a hankering to try Robie Creek as a runner, then by all means, go for it. There are many people who do the Race to Robie Creek as a way to get in shape in the spring, and they may not run another half-marathon the rest of the year. Please see the Race to Robie Creek web site for more information about the race: www.robiecreek.com. Be sure to get out on the course and train before the race. See page 18 for more background about the race and expert tips.

Directions: Head out on Reserve Street and head northeast for Shaw Mountain Road. Take a 90-degree right-hand turn on Shaw Mountain Road and climb for 1.6 miles to a three-way junction with Shaw Mountain Road, Table Rock and Rocky Canyon Road. Go straight on Rocky Canyon and follow the narrow paved road down into Rocky Canyon itself. It's a half-mile of descent and then you'll climb up to a flat spot in the road at mile 3. Now the climb on the dirt road begins in earnest. You'll pass by Five Mile Creek at mile 5.3 and Orchard Gulch at 6.6 - two other areas where the gradient is reasonable. At mile 8, you'll reach Aldape Summit. The climbing is over! Now the grueling downhill begins. You'll go around a couple of sharp switchbacks and cruise down the road. Robie Creek comes in on your left with 1.3 miles left. Hang on and finish at mile 13.

The Hike: Pack plenty of water and food for your journey and have fun.

The Run: Follow the tips from seasoned experts for running the Race to Robie Creek. Training ahead of time will ease the strain on your body. – SS

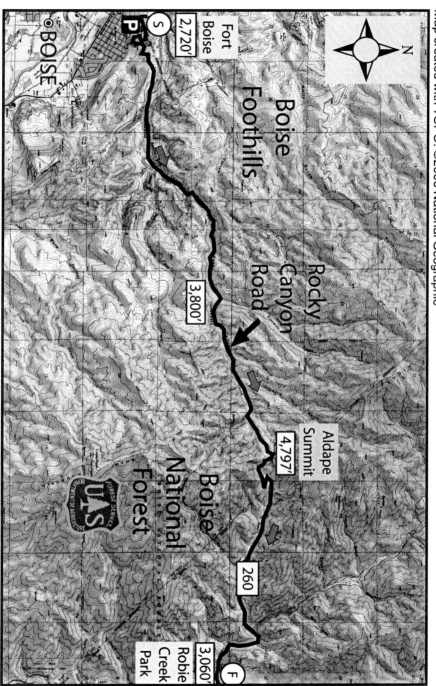

BOISE

Fort
Boise
2,720'

Boise
Foothills

N

Rocky
Canyon
Road

3,800'

Aldape
Summit
4,797'

Boise
National
Forest

U.S.
FOREST SERVICE
DEPARTMENT OF AGRICULTURE

260

3,060'
Robie
Creek
Park

175

#72 Rocky Canyon - Trail #4 Loop

Location: Northeast Boise Foothills
Difficulty: Epic
Distance: 16 miles
Tread: Dirt road, singletrack
Hiking time: 8 hours
Running time: 4 hours
Vertical gain/loss: 3,218 feet/3,318 feet
Watch out for: Speeding vehicles and
other trail users
Water: Seasonal in Cottonwood Creek
and Hulls Gulch
Season: May-October

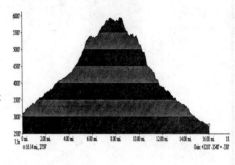

Getting there: From downtown Boise, take State Street east to Fort Street. Take an immediate left on Reserve Street. Follow Reserve to Shaw Mountain Road and follow the road to the top of the grade, and bear left on Rocky Canyon Road. Stay on the paved road to a circular turn-around at the end of the pavement. The hike/run starts here.
Shuttle: Leave a vehicle at the end of N. 9th Street or at Camelsback Park.

General remarks: This is a great long loop for runners and hikers who yearn to climb major vertical (3,218 feet) and test their endurance. Watch for vehicles as you climb Rocky Canyon Road. Once you turn onto the Boise Ridge Road, you won't see many people for the next hour or so. It's a very steep grade up the ridge road for a couple miles, and then when you peel off on Trail #4, it's a long downhill back to Camelsback. Be sure to pack plenty of food and water for this one.

Directions: From the pullout, head up Rocky Canyon Road for 5 increasingly challenging miles to Aldape Summit. Turn left at Aldape and climb an even steeper dirt road for 3.5 agonizing miles. The road climbs along the top of the Boise Ridge, providing great views in all directions. Eventually, the grade will level out, and you'll see a left-hand signed turnoff for Trail #4 at mile 8.5. Go left and plunge down Trail #4, a dished-out motorcycle trail that can be quite sandy in places. You'll peel right at the junction with Trail #6 and stay on Trail #4 down to Sidewinder junction. Turn left on Sidewinder #24 and follow that down to Crestline, Kestrel and Owls Roost back to Camelsback Park. As an alternative, you could take Trail #6 and Trail #5 back to Shane's Trail and then drop into Rocky Canyon from there, saving the need to shuttle. However, there will be more climbing from Trail #5 over to Shane's.

Hike/run notes: Unless you're training for a major hike or run, this route won't be much fun. It's designed to hurt you and punish you and get you ready for lots of climbing and descending over big miles. That said, if you're capable of running this route, then it's got to feel pretty darn good to be that tough and strong. – SS

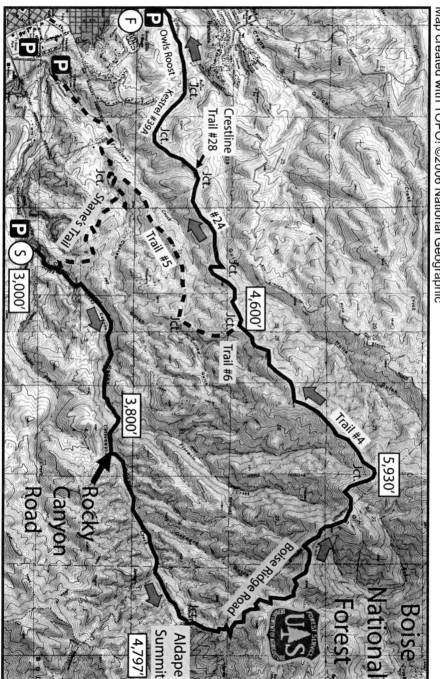

#73 Squaw Creek - Trail #8 - Trail E Loop

Location: East Boise Foothills
Difficulty: Epic gonzo
Distance: 12.7 miles
Tread: Dirt two-track
Hiking time: 5+ hours
Running time: 3 hours
Vertical gain/loss: 3,158 feet
Watch out for: Wildlife and wildflowers trucks and ATVs
Water: Possible rain water in potholes, isolated mountain springs
Season: May - October

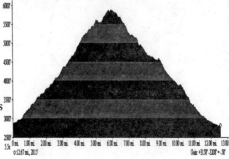

Getting there: In downtown Boise, take Warm Springs Avenue several miles east of town to Harris Ranch. Go straight at Eckert Road and then turn left on Council Springs. Proceed to the trailhead at the dead end. The hike/run starts here. **Shuttle**: Drop a vehicle in the Crow Inn parking lot at the finish area.

General notes: This is a steep-mountain training route that's guaranteed to hurt. I wouldn't recommend this hike/run for fun. Climbing on Trail #8 is steeper than approaching from Trail E, so doing the route clockwise will put all of the agony on the frontside of the workout, and the downhill should be fun. Note that the Boise River Wildlife Management Area is dedicated to protecting wintering deer and elk herds, so the area is closed to public use between Dec. 1 and April 15. Be sure to pack plenty of food and water.

Directions: Head up Squaw Creek Trail #12. It climbs at a steep clip right off the bat for less than a mile. It levels off and climbs again over several heinous pitches to an initial summit at mile 2.2. Here's your junction with Trail #8. Now you've got 2,000 more vertical feet of climbing over just 4 miles. Ouch! It's nasty and it doesn't let up until you get close to Shaw Mountain and Lucky Peak. Trail #8 reaches an initial ridgetop summit, wraps behind Shaw Mountain into the timber briefly and then connects with the road to Lucky Peak, Trail E. Take a hard right and climb the remaining 300 vertical feet to the peak. In the fall, raptor and songbird experts may be trapping and banding birds there. Now it's a long continuous downhill on Trail E. Go left on Trail #9, a softer two-track, to add a side loop to the trip, if you wish. Below the second junction with Trail #9, it's .5 miles to the end of Trail E. Turn left and go less than ½ mile to a junction with Trail #11, a singletrack on your right. Peel off on Trail #11 and cruise 2.5 miles downhill to the Crow Inn. You made it!

The Hike: Don't let the mileage fool you. This is a gonzo climber's special. You'll gain elevation quickly, but the pain factor is high.

The Run: Only super-strong, super-human mountain runners should attempt this route, and that's why I'm including it in the book – just for them. – SS

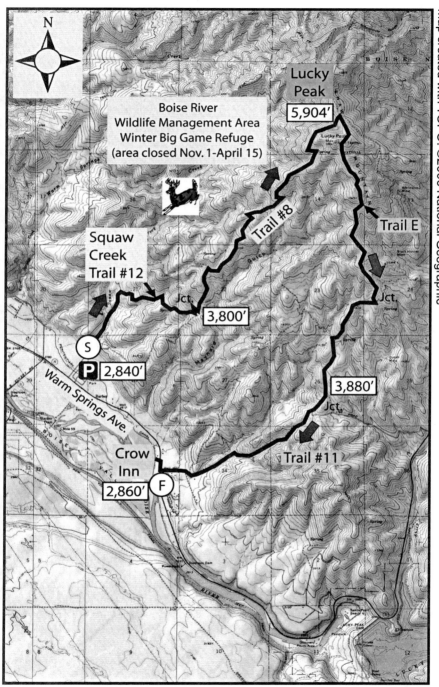

Map created with TOPO! ©2006 National Geographic

179

#74 Thorn Butte-Cottonwood Cr. Loop

Location: Boise National Forest, adjacent to Arrowrock Reservoir
Difficulty: Strenuous to gonzo
Distance: 21.75 miles
Tread: 4WD road, singletrack
Hiking time: 9-11 hours
Running time: 4+ hours
Vertical gain: 3,835 feet
Watch out for: Wildlife, stream crossings
Water: Dependable in Cottonwood Creek
Season: May - October

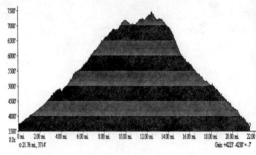

Getting there: From downtown Boise, take Warm Springs Ave. east to Idaho 21. Follow Idaho 21 about 16 miles to the Mores Creek high bridge. Turn right on Forest Service Road #268, the road to Spring Shores Marina. Drive 15 miles along Lucky Peak and Arrowrock to a junction with Forest Road #377. Turn left and follow #377 about 3 miles to the Cottonwood Creek Trailhead on the right. The hike/run starts here.

General notes: This is a variation on the Cottonwood Creek out-and-back route that is longer, but the climb on this route involves hiking/running up a 4WD road to Thorn Butte Lookout. The gradient of the road is much more moderate than scaling the creek trail, and you hike/run down the creek instead. Still, the entire route is close to the length of a marathon, so it's only for the strongest and experienced hikers and runners. Be sure to pack plenty of food and drink.

Directions: Start by climbing Forest Road #377 about four miles on a steep gradient to a four-way saddle junction. Turn right on Forest Road #203 and head up the 4WD road. The grade gets more moderate. At mile 8, the road gets rockier and steeper, as it climbs toward a high ridge. At mile 10.8, Thorn Butte Lookout comes into view. At mile 12, you'll pass by the junction with Cottonwood Creek Trail #189, a singletrack. Here, you can take an optional 500-foot .6-mile climb to the top of the Lookout, or turn right and head down Cottonwood Creek Trail. You'll encounter several bogs and minor creek crossings in the first couple miles. Get used to wet feet – there'll be more than 20 crossings in all before you reach the trailhead.

The Hike: This is a mondo hike that's not suitable for most people. The mileage can be cut back by parking at the saddle junction, and hike up the Thorn Butte Lookout road #203 for as long as you wish and head back. The full 21.75-mile trip is an epic day. You could bring a backpack and make it a two-day trip - much nicer option.

The Run: Anyone who enjoys the Cottonwood Creek out-and-back run has to try this one. It's 9.7 miles and 3,000 vertical feet to the top and a steep descent. – SS

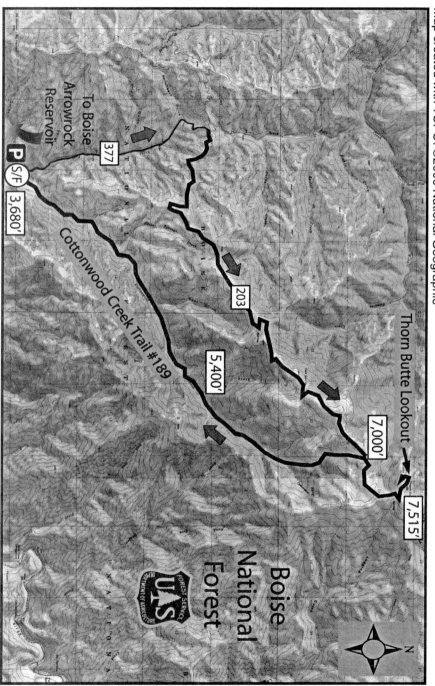

Map created with TOPO! ©2006 National Geographic

Boise National Forest

Thorn Butte Lookout

To Boise
Arrowrock Reservoir

377

203

Cottonwood Creek Trail #189

P S/F 3,680'

5,400'

7,000'

7,515'

N

181

#75 Wilson Creek-Mini Moab Loop

Location: Owyhee Mountains,
south of Nampa
Difficulty: Epic
Distance: 15.6 miles
Tread: Dirt road, singletrack
Hiking time: 7 hours
Running time: 2:45
Vertical gain/loss: 3,158 feet
Watch out for: Wildflowers, wildlife
Water: Seasonal in Wilson Creek;
otherwise it's a dry route.
Season: April-November

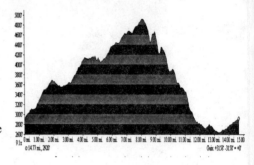

Getting there: From downtown Boise, hook up with I-184 west and head for Nampa. Take the Franklin Road exit (City Center) in Nampa, and turn left. Follow Franklin to the intersection with 11th Street. Turn right and take 11th into downtown Nampa. Follow signs for Idaho 45 south. Take ID 45 to Walters Ferry at the Snake River and turn right on ID 78, heading for Marsing. In a couple miles, turn left on Wilson Creek Road. Proceed up the road to a BLM parking area on the left. The hike/run starts here.

General notes: This is a major hike/run in the foothills of the Owyhee Mountains, about 45 minutes from Boise. Get an early start and power-walk it or run it before it gets too hot. The trail weaves through many cool rock formations on the way over the saddle of Wilson Butte, including a number of hoodoos and spires. The downhill turns unexpectedly into some steep uphill sections, and it also features major large rocks, so footing can be tricky. Bring your camera, plenty of water and a lunch.

Directions: To begin, climb up the Wilson Creek road. It starts out at a steep pitch and then mellows a bit at mile 2. At mile 3.3, ignore the two-track on the left, cross the creek and climb. At mile 4.5, ignore the two-track on the right and go straight. At mile 6.5, turn left on a two-track primitive road and climb to the Wilson Creek saddle (mile 9). Climb to the peak if you wish. Find a lunch spot. Continuing on, the trail drops down and then climbs at a steep pitch against the mountain. Drop down a bit, and you'll come to a three-way junction. Take the middle route, a steep dropoff. Follow the 4WD road as it bounds down the mountain like a mountain goat. At mile 14, you'll drop out of the rocks onto a sandy Pigeon Creek Road. Watch for a two-track on the left, Trail #400. Go west and climb through the sagebrush to a small saddle. Here you can take #300 or #400 over to Wilson Creek Road, finishing at mile 15.6.

The Hike: It's a long hike, but if you've got the whole day, it's a great tour.

The Run: This is a tough running route, more than a half-marathon in distance and more than 3,000 feet of vertical gain. The pain factor is going to be high. – SS

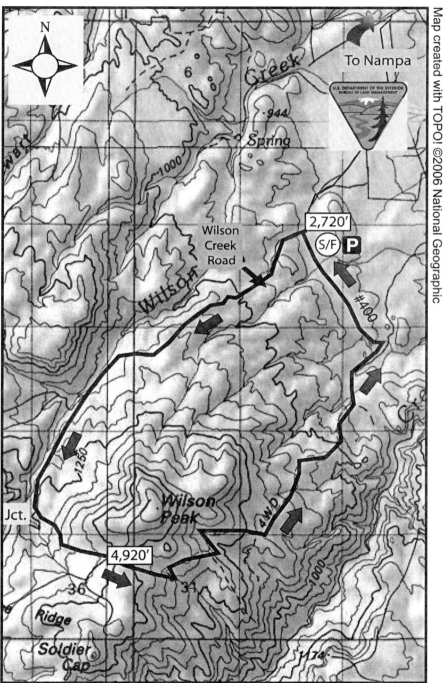

Advertising Gallery

**Please support
the following businesses
because they support you.**

Great People...
Great Service...
A Passion For Running
and Walking

Shu's IDAHO RUNNING CO.

Let us analyze your feet
with our computerized foot
imaging system!

Bring this book/page into the store to receive
$10 off any regularly priced item of $50 or more

Stop by and discover why Runner's
World voted us #1 Running Store
in the Pacific Northwest
and #2 in the Nation!

RUNNER'S WORLD

runner's
choice
award
2007

BEST IN GENERAL EXCELLENCE ★ PACIFIC NORTHWEST

Shu's Idaho Running Company 1758 W. State Street, Boise 83702   208-344-6604
Mon-Fri 10-6 Sat 10-5   www.idahorunningcompany.com

MAKE EVERY DAY
AN ADVENTURE.

REI
8300 West Emerald
Boise, ID

www.rei.com/boise

REI has the Gear and Apparel for all your
Hiking and Trail Running Adventures!

Notes

Notes

Notes